PEOPLE AT ODDS

INDIA AND PAKISTAN

PEOPLE AT ODDS

PEOPLE AT ODDS

INDIA AND PAKISTAN

Heather Lehr Wagner

Chelsea House Publishers
Philadelphia

CHELSEA HOUSE PUBLISHERS

EDITOR IN CHIEF Sally Cheney
DIRECTOR OF PRODUCTION Kim Shinners
CREATIVE MANAGER Takeshi Takahashi
MANUFACTURING MANAGER Diann Grasse

Staff for **INDIA AND PAKISTAN**

ASSISTANT EDITOR Susan Naab
PICTURE RESEARCHER Sarah Bloom
PRODUCTION ASSISTANT Jaimie Winkler
COVER AND SERIES DESIGNER Keith Trego
LAYOUT 21st Century Publishing and Communications, Inc.

http://www.chelseahouse.com

First Printing

1 3 5 7 9 8 6 4 2

Library of Congress Cataloging-in-Publication Data

Wagner, Heather Lehr.
    India and Pakistan / by Heather Lehr Wagner.
        p. cm. — (People at odds.) (People at odds)
Includes bibliographical references and index.
    ISBN 0-7910-6709-2
    1. India—History—Partition, 1947. 2. India—Foreign relations—
Pakistan. 3. Pakistan—Foreign relations—India. I. Title. II. Series.
III. Series: People at odds
DS480.842 .W33 2002
954.03'5—dc21

2002000986

CONTENTS

1

A Separate Peace

For five weeks, Sir Cyril Radcliffe had been hard at work in an unbearably hot Indian cottage. It was July in Delhi, and Radcliffe was wearing clothes better suited to England than the suffocating Indian climate. But there was no time to send for more appropriate clothing. There was barely time for Radcliffe to eat or sleep. The 48-year-old British lawyer was too busy spending his days and most of his nights carving up the most important piece in the British Empire.

In July of 1947, Sir Cyril Radcliffe faced an impossible task: creating two countries from one. To do this, he had to separate 88 million people and divide 175,000 square miles of land. It was a job that the United Nations had refused, and one that Radcliffe accepted only reluctantly. It should have taken months, if not years, but Radcliffe was given only 36 days.

Shown here is a map of the region.

Lord Louis Mountbatten served as the last British Viceroy of India. In 1947, he presided over the division of this prized part of the British Empire into two independent nations—India (predominantly Hindu) and Pakistan (predominantly Muslim).

Cyril Radcliffe was one of the most respected attorneys in England. He served as director-general of the Ministry of Information, had been educated at Oxford, and was a colleague of Lord Mountbatten, the Viceroy of India (Britain's official governor of the Indian peninsula). But Radcliffe had never been to India and there was little time to get to know the vast subcontinent now.

At first, Radcliffe's unfamiliarity with the land he was charged with carving up was thought to be an asset. The various religious communities who populated India had joined together in a successful campaign to drive out Britain and achieve their independence, but the thrill of this victory soon gave way to fierce violence. The minority Muslim community (comprising approximately 20 percent of India's total population) feared what a nation dominated by Hindus would mean for them. The political voice of the Muslim community, Mohammed Ali Jinnah, soon made it clear that the Muslim population would not support an independent nation with a Hindu majority. Violence increased, and soon both British and Indian leaders were left with a worst-case scenario: carve the subcontinent into two nations—one Muslim, one Hindu—or face a civil war.

Those familiar with the politics and the players at work in India could not help but be prejudiced. Some favored the charismatic leader of the Indian Congress party, Jawaharlal Nehru, and his attempts to hold India together. Others saw the wisdom of attempting to appease both sides by offering the two religious communities their separate territories. This is where Cyril Radcliffe was brought in. Known and respected by both Jinnah and Nehru, as well as by the governing British authorities, Radcliffe seemed an unbiased and appropriate choice.

Initially, Radcliffe had been brought to India on a false promise. He had believed that his task in Delhi would be to settle boundary disputes as they arose in certain territories, determining whether selected districts more appropriately belonged to India or to the newly created Muslim land to be known as Pakistan. His superiors in London had lured him with the understanding that he would be given six months to settle these disagreements. It was not until after he had unpacked his suitcases that he learned that his task would be far more monumental—to divide into two a land and a people that had been united for nearly a thousand years and to do so in 36 days.

Radcliffe worked day and night, studying out-of-date census figures, looking at maps, examining charts, trying to determine how the location of industries, rivers and roads would impact any possible divisions. A group of eight judges was assigned to assist him, but their own prejudices (four were Hindu, four were Muslim) made it impossible for them to reach a consensus. Radcliffe had the deciding vote, and the only voice that counted.

Lacking the time to travel to the regions he would soon divide and forever change, Radcliffe instead invited their representatives to come to him. Papers and people from different interest groups (Nehru's Congress Party, Jinnah's Muslim League, Sikh members from the disputed territory of Punjab's Legislative Assembly, and others) were placed before him as he frantically worked to make sense of the often-conflicting data. In the broadest sense, he was working to create Muslim territory where Muslims formed the majority of the population. Prior to his arrival, it had been decided that the new state of Pakistan (from the Urdu word for "Land of the Pure") would, in reality, be two separate territories, formed by dividing the provinces of Punjab (in the northwest corner of India) and Bengal (in the northeast corner). These territories contained large Muslim populations, but lay on opposite sides of the Indian subcontinent, separated by a vast stretch of land that was to remain part of independent India.

For Radcliffe, the task was to draw thousands of miles of borders that would separate states, regions, even villages and even neighborhoods that had once been united. While religion was understood to be a significant factor in his decision-making, other elements also had to be considered. How would critical railroads, roads, power lines and irrigation systems be affected by the separation? Borders, particularly in densely populated areas like Punjab and Bengal, might cut through a farmer's fields or place a factory on the opposite side of the border from its storage facilities or workers.

Which country would be awarded prize cities like Lahore and Calcutta? If the Punjab region was cut off from British-designed sources of water—the valuable irrigation system of canals—how would it continue to play a vital role in producing crops for the region? What impact would the division of India have on the Sikh community, many of whose holiest shrines would soon pass into Muslim hands?

As Radcliffe studied the massive and often-conflicting data, rumors seeped out of the impact that partition (as it was commonly known) might have. Panic quickly followed, as once peaceful communities began to look at their neighbors not as fellow Indians joined together against the British occupiers, but instead as members of the religious majority or minority. In disputed areas, like the Punjab, thousands were killed and thousands more injured as the August deadline for a decision approached. Violence by Hindus against Muslims sparked an even

One of the most difficult tasks in carving two new nations from one was the allocation of resources. Access to the Ganges River (shown here), possession of prize cities, and control of holy shrines were all critical issues in drawing the geographic boundaries of India and Pakistan.

stronger response from Muslims against Hindus, and the killing quickly escalated.

Near the soon-to-be-drawn border, people waited to see where the boundaries would be and hoped to find themselves on the right side of that line. But in certain territories further back from the border, where it was clear that Muslims or Hindus were in the majority, families who found that their religion would soon label them as "enemies" began to pack up their belongings and prepare to evacuate.

The stories that would emerge from this massive migration, as millions faced the prospect of leaving home, friends and even family to cross over a yet-to-be-drawn border, are heartbreaking. Violence was common, as long lines of Muslims heading toward Pakistan would often be separated by only a narrow stretch of land from an equally long line of Hindus heading for India. Frequently these columns of refugees would arrive in their new homeland with nowhere to go, no one to welcome them and no way to earn a living. The impact of partition would be devastating.

A LAND DIVIDED

As Radcliffe neared the end of his task, he came under increasing pressure to provide some hint of his findings, in part for security reasons. The governors of disputed regions were anxious to know exactly where the borders would be drawn so that they could order additional police forces to places where violence would certainly break out once the decision was announced. But even with a few days' advance warning, the troops were simply too small and too widely scattered to maintain the peace.

On August 13, Radcliffe at last completed his task. The final line was drawn, the final boundary noted on his last map. But the British Viceroy Mountbatten, understanding that violence would inevitably follow the release of the boundary information, held on to it for two days while India prepared to celebrate its independence, Pakistan prepared to begin its life as a new nation and Britain prepared to leave. Official ceremonies were accompanied by fierce fires dotting the landscape, as Muslims and Hindus burned each other's homes and property. It was becoming clear that independence would be a time of catastrophe as well as celebration, and Mountbatten wanted to make sure that British representatives were well away from the region.

As quickly as he had completed his task, Radcliffe set about packing his bags. He knew that disaster was only hours away. On August 14, the day before independence was officially launched, Radcliffe prepared to leave. On that day, he wrote a hasty note to his stepson, admitting that, "There will be roughly 80 million people with a grievance who will begin looking for me. I don't want them to find me." He would leave only a few hours after India achieved independence on August 15, so worried about being assassinated that airline officials were required to make a complete search of the airplane before it took off.

Cyril Radcliffe accepted no payment for his work, nor did he ever return to the land he had forever changed. And perhaps it is just as well. For the borders that Radcliffe helped draft—the lines that divided a people and a subcontinent into two—would create decades of conflict, three wars and millions of refugees. Independence would come for Pakistan and India, but the price would be paid in lost lives and a continuous cycle of violence and fear.

THE JEWEL IN THE CROWN

On August 15, 1947, the British flag was lowered from the flagpoles flying over the subcontinent. The British colors were replaced by the flags for newly independent India and Pakistan, but the process of replacing one system of government with another was not nearly so straightforward. The territory ruled over by British royalty since the mid-1800s was never a single nation, but instead a blend of Hindus, Muslims, Sikhs and other religious groups living in vastly different regions, some governed as princely states, others as part of the British crown.

India had served as a kind of cultural and religious melting pot for centuries. Since 2500 B.C., civilizations had developed in the subcontinent, first around the Indus River and then centered at the Ganges River Valley. A culture based on agriculture and trade flourished and then declined as invaders swept into the territory. Tiny kingdoms were united in the 4th and 5th centuries A.D. as part of the Gupta Dynasty, when Hindu culture began to dominate the region. The influence of Islam came later, first with the arrival of the creation of sultanates (kingdoms) in Delhi by Turkish and Afghan invaders in the 10th and 11th centuries, and a few centuries later, with the arrival of Genghis Khan and his invading force. From the 11th to the 15th centuries, Hindu and Muslim cultures coexisted in the region, influencing each other through the mingling of ideas, customs and people.

The arrival of the British in the region brought a new

After nearly a century of British rule, the ethnically diverse region attained independence in 1947. This newfound freedom from colonial rule heightened the cultural conflicts between the Hindu majority and Muslim minority.

era to India. The first British base was established in 1619 on the northwestern coast, but it was the arrival of the British East India Company, a group focusing on establishing trade with the region, that would forever alter India's history. By the late 1600s, the East India Company had established trading stations at Bombay,

Calcutta and Madras, operating through the cooperation and influence of the local princes who ruled over each of these territories.

Chaos dominated the region as the princes gained and lost influence and people shifted their allegiance from one ruler to the next. The East India Company used the confusion to its advantage, gaining influence through their ability to provide employment and goods. Less than 200 years after their arrival in the region, the East India Company essentially ruled over most of India. In 1857, northern Indians launched a rebellion and Britain, fearing the loss of its valuable trading partner, quickly determined to step in. Power was shifted from the East India Company to Britain itself, which began to govern all of India, either through direct rule or through treaties with the remaining local princes friendly to British interests.

For several decades, the British Empire, the dominant military and political power in the world at that time, ruled over vast portions of the Middle East, Asia and Africa. India was considered to be the "jewel in the crown"— the most valuable part of the empire, both strategically and economically. But as the 19th century gave way to the 20th century, rumblings of discontent in the empire grew louder. The British government was frequently oppressive, and its governors enjoyed princely lifestyles while the people they ruled over lived in crippling poverty.

As World War I began, citizens from all corners of the British Empire were drafted to serve in the British army and many served proudly and honorably. But as the war ended, they found themselves once more reduced to the status of second-class citizens, sparking discontent at a time when Britain found itself economically challenged to continue to govern and police such vastly different and far-flung territories.

Rebellion was inevitable, and independence movements

were launched in Ireland, in the Middle East, and in India. In 1920, a British-trained lawyer named Mohandas Gandhi shaped the Indian National Congress party into a mass movement that would ultimately sweep the British out of India. Gandhi's goals were to achieve India's independence through legal means and, when these failed, through non-violent non-cooperation. Gandhi's belief was that if Indians peacefully resisted the British—by refusing to obey laws they felt were unjust or ceasing to work, but never striking back in violence, even when violence was used against them—the justness of their cause would be clear. Gandhi was skilled at using the media and at symbolic gestures, and as he had guessed, world opinion soon weighed heavily against Britain's forceful and often heavy-handed attempts to cling to its Indian territory.

Under Gandhi, Hindus and Muslims united to achieve their independence, but as their goal came nearer the divisions between the two groups grew greater. Gandhi was unable to contain the violence that flared between the two communities as each feared what a newly independent government, freed from the traditional British administration, might mean. The Congress Party leader, Jawaharlal Nehru, firmly believed that India should stand together as an independent and unified nation. The leader of the Muslim League, Mohammed Ali Jinnah, feared that an independent India dominated by Hindus would be worse for Muslims than an India governed by Britain. Through a series of secret negotiations, Jinnah was able to win from the British a promise that two states, not one, would be created when Britain left the subcontinent. With a pending deadline and increasing pressure from both sides, the feverish work of Cyril Radcliffe began.

India's independence came largely through the tireless efforts of Mohandas Gandhi, seen here (at right) conferring with Congress Party leader Jawarhalal Nehru. Nehru went on to become India's first prime minister.

THE NIGHTMARE OF PARTITION

On August 16, 1947, one day after independence was achieved, the former viceroy, now Earl Mountbatten, presented representatives from India and Pakistan with the details of the newly drawn boundaries separating their two nations. Each side was given two hours to read the documents and then return for a second meeting.

As expected, both sides were outraged by what they saw. Each group saw the injustices of seemingly random decisions awarding territory to one or the other nation. One of the most important aspects was the fate of the district of Gurdaspur, in the northern part of the Punjab. Gurdaspur contained a Muslim majority, but it had tremendous strategic significance, as within it ran the only Indian land route into valuable Kashmir. And through Kashmir ran the three rivers that would flow into Pakistan and provide it with the valuable source of water to sustain life in the new nation. If Gurdaspur was awarded to India, the western part of Pakistan (to be known as West Pakistan) would be surrounded by Indian territory and therefore dependent on Indian water for its economic survival. Pakistan might not survive without its valuable link to Kashmir.

Initial reports had indicated that Radcliffe's map awarded Gurdaspur to Pakistan, in keeping with its Muslim majority, but when the final documents were produced on August 16, the region was now part of India. The Pakistani delegation was outraged, believing that Radcliffe had been pressured at the last minute to change his border. But there was little they could do. As part of their agreement, both sides had promised to abide by whatever borders Radcliffe created. And so all groups left the meeting bitterly disappointed. The Sikh community was horrified to discover that many of their sacred places were now in Pakistan. Muslims were dismayed to learn that several of the regions where they were in the majority had been awarded to India.

As the news of the boundaries began to seep out into the streets, uncertainty and fear gave way to complete chaos. Policemen, just like the rest of the population, identified themselves as Muslims, Hindus or Sikhs, and in many cases they found themselves trying to maintain the peace in a village or town that was no longer friendly to them or others of their religion. In certain disputed areas, both the Indian and Pakistani flags had been raised on Independence Day, as uncertainty about the fate of the region dominated. But with the release of the final borders, disaster loomed. Neighbor turned against neighbor, and each incident sparked an even greater spiral of violence in response.

Approximately 12 million people fled to the borders as the details of the partition moved from rumor to reality— a migration dominated by terror and violence. The columns of refugees stretched for miles, as people seized what they could carry of their possessions and frantically rushed to get across the border. Fighting broke out whenever a group of refugees heading in one direction would cross the path of a group heading the opposite way, and soon the trail was littered with the dead and the dying. Trains packed with fleeing people, many clinging to the sides or roof of the railroad cars, would often arrive filled with dead bodies, the victims having been massacred on the way to their destination.

While violence claimed hundreds of thousands of victims, disease and exhaustion claimed more. Spending days on foot, with little food or water and packed together in close quarters, those who had not been attacked by their former countrymen were attacked instead by the brutal conditions.

In the end, the independence of India and the creation of Pakistan would not be remembered by those who had experienced them as a time of great joy and celebration. Instead, they would be remembered with horror and despair—a time when a land truly was sliced into pieces. Approximately one million people died during those initial weeks of independence. And their deaths would mark not an end, but rather a beginning.

As the British hastily created borders and then left, as

The partitioning of India and Pakistan was plagued by rumor, panic, and violence as 12 million Muslim refugees crowded to the newly defined border. In this chaotic scene, trains packed with refugees, many riding on the roofs of railcars, streamed into Pakistan.

religious communities erupted in violence, the history of the subcontinent had entered a new phase. India and Pakistan would exist, independent and separate. But they would be linked in an ongoing cycle of violence, with increasingly sophisticated and deadly weapons at their disposal.

KASHMIR

Much of the conflict that has marked the history of India and Pakistan centers around the region known as Kashmir. Kashmir is located along India's northernmost point and on the eastern corner of Pakistan. Its strategic importance is clear, touching as it does upon borders with China and Tibet, and bisected by the Indus River.

Kashmir is a large valley, surrounded by the snow-capped Himalayan Mountains. These mountains provide Kashmir with a source of clear water when the snows melt and run down into the valley in spring, and are also a formidable barrier, difficult to climb.

Kashmir's rich history dates back to Neolithic times. Excavations in the region have yielded pit dwellings that date back to 3000 B.C., as well as a treasure of stone axes and many tools made of bone.

Women traditionally played an unusually powerful role in Kashmiri society and politics. Queens ruled the land on several occasions, and in ancient Kashmir women were allowed to own private property and manage their own lands. They were not required to wear the traditional Muslim veil.

Kashmir's agricultural riches made it a wealthy territory. It produced saffron (the only state in India to produce this vital ingredient in Indian cooking). It produced fruit and raw wool, both valuable exports.

Its capital, Srinagar, had an equally rich history. Important communities had occupied the space since 300 B.C., although under different names. Since these ancient times, the area of Srinagar (then called Pravarapura) had been famous for its population of scholars, known as Pandits, who traveled from India and China to study the libraries of Sanskrit manuscripts found in the temples and in the private collections of wealthy families.

In 1339, Kashmir changed from a Hindu to a Muslim state under the rule of Sultan Shahabuddin. For the next 500 years, Kashmir would remain under Muslim rule, until it was conquered by Sikh armies in the early 1800s. Sikhs ruled the region—and most of the Punjab—until the 1830s, when they began a series of bloody battles with British forces that had moved into the region. Britain eventually defeated the Sikhs, but rather than seizing all of their land, only took some and set up the rest as a series of princely states, to be ruled by a monarch friendly to British interests.

When India and Pakistan gained their independence, Kashmir became a source of dispute, the conflict deepening when Kashmir became part of India in October 1947. The question of Kashmir has never been fully resolved. The beautiful region had become the site of two wars between India and Pakistan and numerous military incursions.

To this day, the conflict continues, as Kashmiri rebels maintain their efforts to gain their own independent state of Kashmir or a union with Pakistan.

An Uncivil War

For Muhammad Ali Jinnah, August 11, 1947, marked the beginning of an exciting new era, both in his life and in the life of the nation he had helped to create. On that Monday, at the first meeting of the Pakistan constituent assembly, he was unanimously elected Pakistan's first president.

Those who had accused Jinnah of being responsible for the anti-Hindu violence that had marked the last few months and who believed that Pakistan would be a strictly Islamic nation would have been surprised to hear the new president's first speech before the assembly:

> You are free; you are free to go to your temples, you are free to go to your mosques or to any other place of worship in this State of Pakistan. . . . You may belong to any religious caste or creed—that has nothing to do with the business of the State. . . . You will find that in the course of time Hindus would cease to be Hindus and Muslims would cease to be Muslims, not in the religious sense, because that is the personal faith of each individual, but in the political sense—as citizens of the nation.

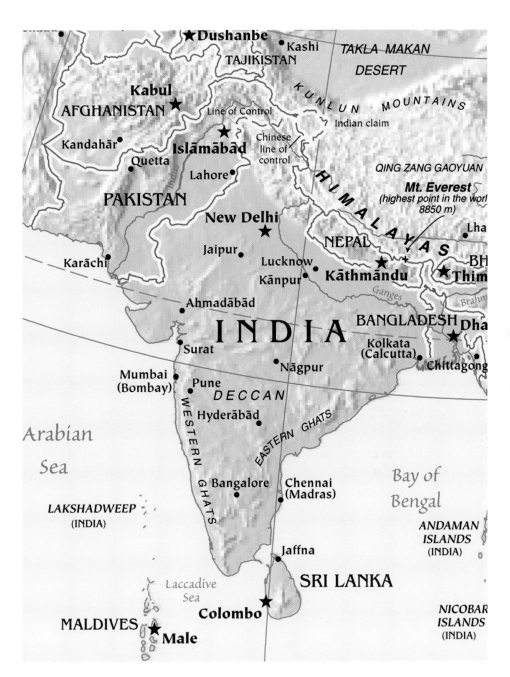

The complex religious and ethnic divisions between India and Pakistan made the borders between the two nations difficult to determine. Resources had to be equitably divided to ensure the economic success of both nations.

It was a dream of a great nation, one founded for religious reasons but would one day offer freedom for many different religions. For the former attorney, who had once been described as the "ambassador of Hindu-Muslim unity," it was a defining moment. Jinnah had little in common with the people he had been elected to lead. He was the son of a wealthy merchant, and had lived a privileged life, studying law in England and serving first as an attorney in Bombay and later as a representative to the All-India Congress. He was always well-dressed and well-spoken, and early in his political career had become passionately involved in the cause of Indian independence. It was only later that he began to advocate creating a separate Muslim territory.

From the late 1930s on, Jinnah became active in the demands for a partition of India, and less than 10 years later, his demands had become reality. As he stood before the crowd on that noteworthy August day, outlining his vision of a secular (non-religious) government, his vision of a great nation rising up from the ashes of partition inspired all who heard.

But his vision of a great nation would quickly be tested. A border dispute in Kashmir would spark a war between India and Pakistan. And the 71-year-old president, already weakened by the stress of the struggle for independence, was ill with tuberculosis. As he proudly assumed the presidency of the newly created Pakistan, he did not know that he had little more than a year to live.

BEYOND INDEPENDENCE

On the other side of the India-Pakistan border, another former lawyer, also educated in England, was mapping out the future of the newly independent nation he had been elected to lead. On August 14, 1947, India has gained its

On August 14, 1947, Jawarhalal Nehru became India's first prime minister. Nehru offered large financial incentives to princes willing to commit their territories to India.

independence, and Jawaharlal Nehru had been chosen its first prime minister. The 57-year-old Nehru had opposed plans to partition India in fierce arguments with Jinnah, his former colleague. But now that partition had become a reality, Nehru began to map out the ways in which he could transform India from a backward colony to a modern nation, one step in the evolution of a society once beholden to generations of British overseers into a contemporary world power.

To move India forward, Nehru first wanted to make certain that all of India was unified. He was concerned by the lingering violence along the newly created borders with Pakistan, and by rumors of disloyalty in certain territories that had been disputed up to the moment that Cyril Radcliffe's boundaries were finally revealed.

Prior to independence, India had been governed under different systems in different territories. Some regions of the subcontinent were under direct British administration; others were considered "princely states." A total of 562 of these princely states had existed under the British system, and their rulers (provided that they were friendly to British interests) were allowed to govern their own territories. As Britain prepared to withdraw from India, the princes were offered the opportunity to choose which country they wished to join—India or Pakistan. For most, the choice was clear, and some princes whose states were located along the border happily accepted Nehru's offer of financial assistance (large annual "allowances" for the rest of their life) and voted to join India.

But a few princes had refused to make the choice, including the Hindu ruler of the northern border state of Kashmir. While Kashmir's ruler was Hindu, the vast majority of his subjects were Muslim. An area of great beauty and strategic importance, nestled in the foothills of the Himalayan Mountains, Kashmir contained the valuable source of the rivers that flowed into Pakistan, responsible for the development of the new nation's agricultural system. But it was also the birthplace of Nehru.

The prince of Kashmir—known as the Maharajah of Kashmir—had stood firm for months, refusing to bend to Nehru's bribes or to the rumblings of his discontented

Muslim population. He proudly announced that Kashmir would join neither Pakistan nor India, but instead would remain its own, independent state. Perhaps he believed that his state could become a kind of melting pot for the region—a Muslim people, ruled by a Hindu, whose borders touched not only India and Pakistan, but also China and Russia.

This claim of independence would be quickly tested. Much of the Muslim population was not pleased with the Maharajah's decision. A group of Kashmiri Muslims, many of whom had once served in the Indian army, announced the formation of an *Azad* (Free) Kashmir Government, and called for the overthrow of the Maharajah. Contacts were made with the Pathan tribes, fierce fighters based along the border. By mid-October they had launched an invasion from Pakistan into Kashmir, labeling it a *jihad*, or holy war.

The fighting was intense, and that Pathans enjoyed several rapid victories, covertly supported by Kashmiri Muslims dissatisfied with the Maharajah's reign. By October 25, the invading force was only a few miles from Srinagar, Kashmir's capital.

At this point, the Maharajah found himself reconsidering the wisdom of independence. He sent a hasty message to the government of India, announcing that he had decided that Kashmir should become part of India, and requesting that Indian troops be dispatched to the region immediately. Nehru did not take long to respond—Indian planes were immediately sent to the airfield at Srinagar, arriving just in time to prevent the invading force from seizing Kashmir's capital.

It is not clear exactly what role Pakistan played in the initial invasion of Kashmir by the Pathan force. Did Jinnah and his other senior government officials actively support the invasion? Did they merely offer silent support, in the hope that Kashmir would soon swing into Pakistani territory? Or did the invasion come as a surprise? Whatever the facts, it is clear that once Jinnah learned that the Maharajah had announced his wish to join India and that Indian troops had been sent to Kashmir to fight off the invading forces, he was furious. He immediately ordered the Pakistani army to move into Kashmir, but senior military officials persuaded him that this was not the wisest decision. The Pakistani army had not even been completely organized yet. Soldiers who had once formed part of the Indian army were now trying to form units and create a new structure for a Pakistani army. The army was still in chaos and was in no shape to mount a serious invasion. Also, the more experienced military leaders knew that, with the current level of tension in Kashmir, an invading Pakistani army would soon find itself at war with India.

Jinnah reluctantly agreed to wait. For several months, Indian forces pushed back the invading forces, while the Pakistani army focused on building up its structure and preparing for combat. By the spring of 1948, the time had come.

Kashmir is a beautiful place in the spring—a stark contrast with the overcrowded streets of Calcutta and Lahore. As the snow from the Himalayan Mountains melts and rushes into the streams and rivers, the area bursts with spring flowers and blossoming fruit trees. But the rich and fertile land soon became the sight of conflict, as Pakistani armies marched over the border. Caught in the crossfire, the Kashmiri people were victims not merely of the incompetence of British officials, seeking a quick solution to the nightmare of Hindu-Muslim conflict, but also of the competing desires of two new nations anxious to cement their strategic positions in this new political system.

It was an unofficial war at first, as Pakistani troops helped the Pathan forces regain some of the northern territory they had lost. But the prized, fertile regions lay beyond their grasp for several months both sides pressed ahead with two goals: seize as much of Kashmir as possible and prevent the fighting from spreading into actual Indian or Pakistani territory. The violence that had barely been contained by the creation of India and Pakistan now sprang to life again, as both sides battled fiercely for a region that had been denied them during partition.

It is important to remember that both armies were led by military commanders who had once fought on the same side as British officers. As spring gave way to summer and then to fall, the leaders of both armies maintained a kind of informal contact. They were experienced enough to understand that they could be committing their men to a war with no easy exit strategy, plenty of environmental hazards as cold weather arrived, and no clear victory in sight. By December of 1948, these commanders had had enough, and through urgent communications to their respective governments, they were able to persuade their leaders of the wisdom of a cease-fire. At India's request, the United Nations stepped in to finalize the cease-fire, basing the terms upon the location of each side's troops when the fighting halted. The cease-fire was formally declared on January 1, 1949, but it would not prove lasting. The boundary line (known as the Line of Control) was arbitrary, a reflection simply of the point where each side had been standing when the fighting stopped. No consideration was given to community ties, language, religion or any of the other links that might place a region on one side or the other of the border. As the military campaign gave way to a political one, the stage was set for future conflict.

But Jinnah would not participate in the diplomatic negotiations. The founder of Pakistan, described by the people as *Quaid-e-Azam*, or "Great Leader," had died, a mere 13 months after his dream of an independent state for Muslims had been realized. His final months had been spent alternating high-level meetings in Lahore with trips to the mountains to attempt to rest and cure the coughing that was weakening his lungs. Doctors soon diagnosed lung cancer as well as tuberculosis.

He spent his last days of life a mere shadow of the once proud man he had been. His weight dropped to 80 pounds, and pneumonia was added to the illnesses he was fighting. On September 11, 1948, as Pakistani troops fought fiercely in Kashmir, their leader was flown to Karachi, where doctors felt the hospital was best able to care for him. From the airport, he was placed in a military ambulance headed for the city, but the ambulance broke down en route. For more than an hour the leader and his entourage waited for another ambulance to arrive. Stranded on the road into Karachi, the heat in the ambulance was overwhelming, and Jinnah lacked the strength to muster even enough energy to brush away the flies buzzing near his face. When a replacement ambulance finally arrived and rushed Jinnah to the hospital, the leader had only a few hours to live. He died at 10:20 P.M.

Jinnah was buried in Karachi, only a short distance from where he had been born. The place where he is buried, marked in stately pink marble, is still visited by citizens of the nation he helped to build. But like his tenure as leader, his vision of a democratic and secular government for Pakistan would be short-lived. It was an extraordinarily difficult task Jinnah set for himself—the

Religious and civil freedoms rarely come without a price. Muhammad Ali Jinnah, the founder and first ruler of Pakistan, suffered from both lung cancer and tuberculosis. Only 13 months after realizing his dream of an independent Muslim state, he died.

job of uniting a diverse group who had never considered themselves one people and whose only common factor was their religion. The Pakistan that survived him would become quite different from the state of which he had dreamed.

THE BEGINNINGS OF INSECURITY

Within one year of partition, both Pakistan and India had found themselves at war. In the aftermath of the cease-fire in Kashmir, India fared much better. Why?

First is the question of leadership. The people on both sides had rallied around their charismatic leaders—men who had a clear vision for their new countries and the connections to make things happen. But with the death of Jinnah, Pakistan lost the great leader who had been able to bring together different groups under a single banner: Muslims. Following Jinnah's death, this definition by religion would prove costly.

Jinnah's trusted number two, Liaquat Ali Khan, stepped into the leadership role, assuming the position of Prime Minister. He was able to hold different groups together, in part because his fairness and integrity were universally respected. But one of his earliest acts sparked unease within the non-Muslim population. As Pakistan took the first tentative steps toward creating a constitution, the Prime Minister made it clear that this critical document would be drafted in keeping with Islamic principles of democracy, freedom and tolerance. The example offered by other Islamic states was not reassuring—in these states, non-Muslims were categorized as *dhimmis*, or second-class citizens.

Concern spread among the non-Muslim population, as well as those who remembered Jinnah's vision of a secular Pakistan. And then, suddenly, a group of high-ranking military officers was arrested and charged with trying to overthrow the government. As the trial proceeded, the news leaked out that they had been planning to set up a military dictatorship.

But the government that had been their target was

After Jinnah's death, Liaquat Ali Khan took over as Pakistan's prime minister. To unite his diverse peoples, he began work to create Pakistan's first constitution. But in October of 1951 he was assassinated by an Afghan terrorist, leaving Pakistan once again in search of a leader.

about to undergo a change independent of their actions. In October of 1951 Liaquat Ali was assassinated by an Afghan terrorist. The reasons for the terrorist's actions were never clear—he was killed on the spot before he could be questioned or brought to trial.

With each small step that Pakistan took, violence or a sudden loss of leadership seemed to push it back. The country suffered further from its location and geography. Because it came into existence divided into two pieces, its borders were not clear and a source of constant dispute. Ethnic groups were caught in the crossfire, divided by arbitrary boundaries and political maneuvering.

When Pakistan was created in 1947, it was the fifth most populous nation in the world. And yet it never was able to seize its rightful place as a large nation. Jinnah's focus at the beginning had been on nation building, and Pakistan never moved to a stage where it could reach out to other nations and begin to form international alliances. In part, its creation as a kind of "alternative to India" left it constantly struggling to prove itself, constantly worrying about border incursions and holding together the divided portions of its territory. Rather than creating a strong national identity, its earliest identity became "not India." Unable to look outward, Pakistan spent these crucial early years marked by in-fighting, border disputes, and quarrels about the role Islam should play in the new government. It was a missed opportunity that future generations of Pakistanis would come to regret.

NEHRU'S LEADERSHIP

India grappled with its own problems, forming its own constitution and dealing with the refugee problem created by the partition line, but the continuous leadership of Nehru ensured a greater stability on the Indian side of the border. Nehru was not without critics or rivals for the leadership position, but his experience in foreign affairs defined him as India's leader both within and outside its borders. His focus in the beginning had been on social issues, building a role for India within Asia, and he was remarkably astute at forming relationships with just the right person at the right time.

In the early months of India's independence, Nehru was heavily influenced by the opinions of Gandhi, whose success in leading the independence movement had elevated him to near-saint status in India. But Gandhi, as he reached his 78th year, viewed his accomplishments as essentially a failure. While the British were gone, India had been torn in two and still was marked by violence. Hindus and Muslims were locked in a cycle of hostility. Instead of Gandhi's vision of India for Indians, the land had been transformed into India for Hindus and Pakistan for Muslims—and even those two nations had been unable to achieve a peaceful coexistence.

On January 30, 1948, en route to a prayer meeting, Gandhi was assassinated by a young Hindu. This violent end to a peaceful life shocked the nation. It also marked the end of an era. Nehru was now free to make his own decisions, following his own group of advisers rather than the guidance of Gandhi. And India began to move ahead, no longer looking back in sorrow at the failure that led to partition, but instead to a future shaped by the reality of India after independence.

Nehru set to work shaping the Indian Constitution. The result was a principally western document, heavily influenced by European and American constitutions. The government would follow the parliamentary system, but it is particularly interesting to contrast certain points in the constitutions of Pakistan and India. Despite the intense lobbying of certain Hindu groups, the legacy of Gandhi prevailed in drafting a document that proclaimed tolerance for all religions in India. India would be a secular state. The same extremist groups also lobbied intensely to make Hindi the official language of India, but instead, to preserve the workings of a government whose administration had operated in English for years under the British system, it was decided the English would be the official language of the Indian government. For 15 years, it would be so.

As 1949 passed, conflict with Pakistan erupted again, this time on the economic front. India devalued its currency in September of 1949, and requested Pakistan to do the same, in part to make it easier to negotiate a new exchange rate. But Pakistan refused, and the tensions that resulted meant that by December of 1949, both countries stopped trade with each other. The effects were immediate—India stopped coal supplies to Pakistan, claiming that Pakistan had refused to supply planned deliveries of raw jute. The East Bengal region of East Pakistan, a major supplier of raw jute, was left with huge amounts of jute with nowhere to ship it. The mills, located in West Bengal, had no jute to process. As East Pakistan struggled under the sudden economic crisis, unemployed workers turned against each other, using religion as an excuse for their fears. Hindus in East Pakistan, the targets of the violence, headed to India, where the unemployment led these new immigrants to be unwelcome. Meanwhile, out-of-work Muslims from East Pakistan headed for West Pakistan, setting off a refugee crisis in both Pakistan and India that mirrored that of only a few years' earlier.

There were calls for war, but Nehru favored a more moderate approach. He visited the border several times and then announced, in March of 1950, that he was not in favor of either a war or a population exchange as a solution to the crisis. Instead, he invited the Prime Minister of Pakistan, Liaquat Ali Khan, to come to India to meet and work out a more sensible solution.

After the currency devaluation of 1949, India stood on the brink of war with Pakistan. In April of 1950, in an attempt to prevent armed conflict, India's Prime Minister Nehru (left) invited Pakistan's Prime Minister Liaquat Ali Khan (right) to India to work out a diplomatic solution.

The two Prime Ministers held a series of talks on April 2. But while Nehru's position seems reasonable and progressive, it was not popular in India. Many felt that his meeting with Liaquat Ali Khan was anti-Hindu, and that his refusal to lead India into war made the country seem weak and afraid.

Rumblings of discontent and challenges to Nehru's leadership within his own party left him fighting domestic squabbles, rather than focusing on leading India ahead into the future. By August of 1951, he had had enough. He resigned from the Congress Party, a shock to a nation that had viewed him as the only legitimate successor to Gandhi as the father figure of India. The political backlash was so great that members within the Congress Party once more rallied behind Nehru. The Congress president, who had led much of the criticism of Nehru, was forced to resign, and Nehru was elected to succeed him. For the next 10 years, Nehru would hold the joint positions of prime minister and Congress president. It was a power base that would enable him to shape the future of his country.

UNITY FROM POWER

While the government of Pakistan struggled with changing leadership and carving out a new identity, India under Nehru benefited from a kind of comfortable continuity. Nehru had believed in and supported Gandhi's campaign of peaceful resistance, but in the aftermath of independence the administration of India under Nehru differed little with the administration of India under the Viceroy. The luxurious palace of the Viceroy—a building Gandhi had suggested should become a hospital for the poor—became the home of Nehru. India's president strolled the same hallways that its previous rulers had walked; he spent his days surrounded by much of the same privilege and ceremony that had marked the governments of previous British administrators.

While this led India far from the mission Gandhi had envisioned, it provided the land with a sense of continuity and confidence that a superior with special skills was in charge, not a simple man of the people. Nehru's connection to Gandhi provided him with a special status, and he astutely understood that people were most willing to follow not someone just like them, but someone somehow better and special.

One of the cornerstones of Nehru's foreign policy was the idea of nonalignment—remaining independent from foreign alliances and foreign problems. In part, this policy was based on the reality of India's history and geography. India's large size gave it the freedom to make its own choices. Its recent experience under colonial rule left it suspicious of any foreign ties that might, once more, bring a foreign occupier to its soil. Above all else, Nehru identified the principal obstacle to India's development: the overwhelming poverty of such a large portion of its population. Nehru believed that foreign ties, alliances and obligations, would mean a shift in focus to international rather than domestic responsibilities. Nehru wanted the majority of India's revenue to remain within India.

However, Nehru's policy of peaceful nonalignment and announced friendship with all the nations of the world contained one "but." It did not apply to Pakistan.

The Conflict Continues

The meeting between the two Prime Ministers—Nehru and Liaquat—sparked hope that there might ultimately be a peaceful solution to the conflict between India and Pakistan. But both leaders paid the price for their attempt at compromise—Nehru in a series of public and private challenges to his leadership, Liaquat with his life.

The death of the Pakistani Prime Minister in October 1951 at the hands of an Afghan assassin raised many questions. The police officer at the rally who had quickly shot and killed the assassin, an inspector named Mohammad Shah, was questioned extensively, both by Pakistani officials and by representatives from Britain's Scotland Yard, who were called in to assist with the investigation. Mohammad Shah himself was assassinated a few years later, adding to the suspicion that Liaquat's assassin may have been part of a conspiracy amongst high-level Pakistani officials anxious to seize power for themselves. Many of those who had criticized Liaquat's willingness to meet and negotiate with Nehru fell under suspicion.

Long-standing differences are often difficult to resolve quickly. In the Pakistani city of Lahore, all the country's cultural influences are visible. Stores with Punjabi and English signs exist side by side with the tower of an Islamic mosque.

Many foreign observers predicted that the sudden death of two leaders in such a short period of time would mean the end of the young nation of Pakistan, but in fact Liaquat's death sparked almost no universal reaction. There were no outbursts of violence, no public ceremonies mourning the passing of the leader, as had happened when Jinnah died. In a sense, it was as if his leadership had meant little to the people of Pakistan.

And in a sense, this was true. Jinnah's role had been central in the development of Pakistan, but under Liaquat much of the power had shifted from the national government to the regional provinces. Powerful factions had sprung up in the distant parts of the nation, where tribal leaders and influential governors had been busily creating their own centers of authority. Liaqat had not effectively challenged these tiny "mini-governments," and as a result, Pakistan began to slide from a strong, unified nation to a loose coalition of different regions that frequently argued among themselves.

The events of October 1951 demonstrated the different paths India and Pakistan had chosen. India had become an international player, openly criticizing U.S. policy toward Third World countries at the United Nations and, as a result, gaining new attention on the global stage. While militarily India was still developing, its diplomatic skills were already gaining attention. And this made many in Pakistan very nervous.

IN SEARCH OF A LEADER

When news of the prime minister's assassination reached Pakistani officials, they were in agreement on one point: a successor must be found quickly. But the question of who that successor would be was much less clear. Before the dead prime minister's body had even returned to the capital, a series of high-level meetings were held, where different candidates were proposed and rejected. Finally, it was decided Khwaja Nazimuddin, the governor-general of Pakistan, would become the new prime minister. It was an appointment that pleased the citizens of the troubled region of East Bengal—Nazimuddin was one of their own. But it pleased few others.

Nazimuddin inherited a government in crisis. A strong

leader might have been able to face down the challenges of provincial leaders while dealing with concerns about India, but Nazimuddin was not that man. In fact, he failed to even live up to the hope of those in East Bengal who thought this "native son" might bring greater opportunities to the region. Nazimuddin, having spent most of his life in cities, did not speak the native language of his home region—Bangla. His speeches, most often made in English or Urdu, actually had to be translated so that people in his home district could understand them.

In fact, it was the question of language that would spark a disaster in East Bengal. Only a few months after becoming Prime Minister, Nazimuddin decided to visit the region to promote many of the government's new programs. Rather than arriving to cheering supporters, Nazimuddin discovered a hostile crowd that seemed to grow more violent as his speech went on.

Nazimuddin's political platform had been based on unity —the kind of unity that would bring different Pakistanis together and address some of the regional conflict that had made it nearly impossible for a central government to create a national administration. One piece of this plan for unity was a single national language. Nazimuddin noted that Jinnah himself had made a similar decision, feeling that Urdu made the most sense as the common language that could tie together all the pieces of Pakistan and best unify the Muslim community.

For the Bangla-speaking Pakistanis, this was not happy news. Criticism and protests erupted almost immediately, and Nazimuddin was forced to make the weak defense that he was merely voicing government policy, not his own personal views. Student protests in Bengal quickly led to general strikes. Police pleas to students and workers to stop the violence went unanswered, and soon the protestors were throwing bricks at the police, who then responded with tear gas and arrests. But the police were quickly overwhelmed, riots followed, and the military was called in to put down the disturbance. Before the violence had ended, four students died. The date of their death—February 21, 1951—would be from then on known as "Shaheed Day"— the day of the Bengali martyrs. It would become a rallying point for a movement that would ultimately end in the loss of East Pakistan.

Nazimuddin's incompetence in handling the Bengali crisis would soon be mirrored in a far greater disturbance in Punjab. Disagreements between different Muslim factions in the region disintegrated into protests and riots. Disputes centered around one particular faction, the Ahmadis, and they soon became the target of violence. Nazimuddin was unable or unwilling to take quick and decisive action to put down the uprising. Only after the protests had disrupted all activity in Lahore and the surrounding areas, along with many deaths and destruction of property, was the Prime Minister prompted to order martial law throughout the Punjab. By the time order was finally restored, the economy of the Punjab had been devastated and the government fatally weakened. On April 17, 1953, Nazimuddin was told to immediately fire his cabinet and senior officers. Unwilling to comply, he found himself fired instead.

THE INTERNATIONAL QUESTION

The new Prime Minister of Pakistan was also a Bengali, but Mohammad Ali Bogra was an experienced politician and administrator and, above all else, a diplomat. He had been Ambassador to Burma, the High Commissioner in Ottawa, and most recently served as Pakistan's ambassador to the United States. With Bogra's appointment, Pakistan

In an effort to build alliances with western nations, Pakistan's Prime Minister Mohammad Ali Bogra entered his nation into the South-East Asia Treaty Organization (SEATO) in 1955. An experienced diplomat, Bogra knew the value of forging ties with the U.S., Great Britain, Australia, and New Zealand.

would enter a next phase, one in which it sought to strengthen its position through links with other governments, a path quite different from the position of non-alignment Nehru had chosen for India.

In the next few years, Pakistan would begin to build a series of alliances that would serve to position it both within the Muslim world and on the global stage. A treaty with Turkey, following cultural and commercial exchanges, was concluded in 1954, followed by a treaty with Iran. In 1955, Pakistan joined the South-East Asia Treaty Organization whose members include Britain, Australia, New Zealand and the United States. At a time when one corner of the subcontinent (India) was carefully refusing to align itself with anyone else, Pakistan set about studiously forming military and economic alliances with as many western powers as possible.

Despite these international gains, the next three years were a time of internal political chaos in Pakistan. Three prime ministers assumed office, and were then forced to resign. Violence flared in Bengal, where opposition parties were able to have the Speaker of their legislature certified insane. As the Deputy Speaker attempted to take his place, a riot ensued. Pieces of wood were thrown in the fight, fatally striking the Deputy Speaker. It was clear that the system in place had failed miserably.

On October 7, 1958, martial law was declared in Pakistan. Both the national and regional governments were all shut down. All political parties were eliminated. Pakistan's president, Iskander Mirza, announced that a military general, Ayub Khan, would serve as "chief martial law administrator." He might as well have signed his own resignation papers then and there. Within one month, President Mirza had a group of late-night visitors, all members of the military. They made it clear to him that it was in his own best interest to leave Pakistan immediately, and within a few hours he was on a plane bound for England. General Ayub was now in control, both as military administrator and with his new title of president of Pakistan.

Ayub immediately set about to straighten out the chaos. Government jobs were handed over to military men. Politicians remaining in Pakistan were given essentially two choices: agree to immediately retire, or face a military tribunal investigating alleged corruption. Most wisely found early retirement the more attractive option. By the early 1960s, President Ayub had drafted a new constitution that specified the president, rather than the prime minister or any other group of officials, would hold all significant power.

Ayub sought to correct Pakistan's dependency on Indian water. India had proved itself at times unwilling to provide the water on which Pakistan's agriculture depended. Ayub negotiated a new deal—this one with the United States—that gave Pakistan financial and technical support to build a vast hydroelectric and water storage system in northern Pakistan. But Ayub went one step further. He also met with Nehru in September 1960 to carve out a new agreement, known as the Indus Basin agreement, which guaranteed the continued flow of water to Pakistani farmlands.

While the country soon experienced greater economic growth due to the land reforms and development plans Ayub had championed, he found that many of his ideas met with great resistance, particularly among the more traditional Islamic sections of Pakistan. Concerned about the problem of overpopulation, Ayub had attempted to introduce family planning programs on the local level in an effort to limit the size of families. He opposed the practice of Pakistani women wearing the *burqa,* or veil, believing that it limited women's ability to contribute to Pakistan's development. These and other of his more progressive plans sparked protests and criticism from Islamic religious leaders.

The 1960s would bring great change to Pakistan, as a strong leader at last attempted to shape a very different Pakistan from the chaos that had prevailed after its founding. But change was also happening in India— change that would place the two countries once more on a collision course.

A LEADERSHIP CHALLENGE

As India moved into the 1960s, it found itself in an increasingly uncomfortable position, both internationally and domestically. Nehru had consistently worked to place

India at the forefront of developing nations, but as more and more former colonies gained their independence, their leaders were no longer willing to listen to Nehru's lectures and strict guidelines. The Soviet Union and the United States, finding a willing partner in Pakistan, were less eager to court Nehru in the hope of winning strategic position on the subcontinent.

In India, the population had grown explosively, far more quickly than domestic plans had anticipated. Food shortages were common and resources were being stretched on every level. Opposition parties were becoming more vocal in their criticism of the government and its inability to bring large social programs from the planning stage to reality.

But the biggest concern came from the Himalayan border with China, where a dispute over the boundaries soon led to war. India's policy of nonalignment became more of a guideline than a rule when it became clear that China was far stronger and more determined than had originally been anticipated. India soon turned to both Britain and the United States for assistance—but this aid came with a price tag. Once the war with China had ended, India began to feel pressure from its allies to settle the dispute with Pakistan over Kashmir, and do it quickly.

Hopes for a peaceful solution were raised when Nehru announced, in November 1962, a meeting with Pakistan's President Ayub to discuss possible solutions to the Kashmir problem. But these hopes were short-lived. Following the meeting, Nehru spoke before the Indian parliament, stating that he would never be willing to change the current status in Kashmir.

It was one of the last strong political stands he would make. He was weakening and, at the age of 74, no longer as eager for the political fights that would keep him in power. The question of who would be his successor had

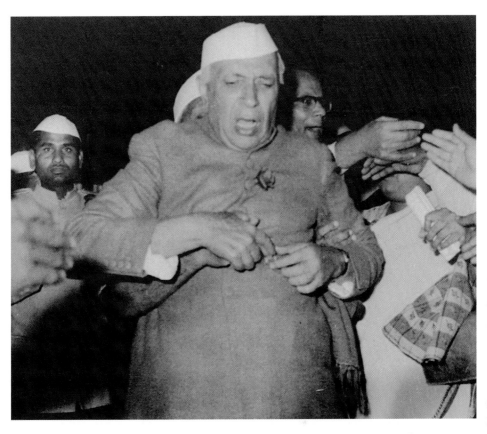

During the early 1960s, India faced diplomatic isolation, overcrowding, and food shortages. Criticism of Prime Minister Nehru grew and violence frequently flared in the streets. Here, the Prime Minister is grabbed by a security officer as a riot erupts.

been whispered for several months. A number of candidates were discussed, including Nehru's daughter, Indira Gandhi, who had served as Nehru's hostess, informal adviser, and more recently, president of the Congress Party. But the question had not been resolved when, on January 8, 1964, Nehru suffered a stroke. Suddenly, India was plunged into intrigue. Nehru's daughter, Indira, closely monitored her father, limiting access to him and giving rise to rumors that he was severely incapacitated and that she was secretly making all decisions herself. As others jostled themselves into the spotlight, the question remained: who would succeed Nehru?

The question had not been answered when trouble began in Kashmir. In December 1963 and January 1964, a series of riots had swept through Srinigar, the capital of Kashmir. They had centered first around the disappearance of a holy relic (one of the hairs from the beard of Mohammed, Islam's prophet) from a mosque, and later, after the relic was found, around the imprisonment of a Kashmir leader, who had been held for 11 years. Both Pakistan and India exchanged heated discussions about the troubles in the United Nations. The United States then put forward a proposal suggesting that the best solution to the crisis might be to make Kashmir independent, a suggestion that was ultimately voted down. But the violence only grew worse, spreading to border towns in India and East Pakistan.

Rumors of war between India and Pakistan grew stronger. To cool the temperature along the border, Nehru decided to release the imprisoned Kashmir leader in April, and then, apparently in better health, he announced plans for a meeting with Pakistan's President Ayub. Tragically, this meeting would not take place. On the day that newspaper headlines printed news of the plans for the meeting—May 27, 1964—Nehru died.

It is interesting to speculate whether or not the Kashmir crisis might have been resolved had Nehru lived long enough to hold the meeting with President Ayub. Both sides had assumes such strident positions on Kashmir that it seems unlikely. But it is certain that India without the leader who had guided it since independence began to move along a different path, one that would lead it into conflict with Pakistan again and again.

THE CONFLICT DEEPENS

Nehru's successor was Lal Bahadur Shastri, an experienced politician who lacked Nehru's desire for peacemaking and the mantle of leadership that might have enabled him to make a significant offer to prompt peace in Kashmir. And politics on the Pakistan side of the border elevated Kashmir to even greater significance.

An election was being held, one that was in many ways a test of President Ayub's popular support. As election day neared, one of Ayub's deputies—a charismatic and ambitious politician named Zulfikar Ali Bhutto—elevated Kashmir to a critical aspect of Ayub's campaign. Bhutto had earned degrees from the University of California at Berkeley and from Oxford, and he was both a skilled diplomat and an outstanding speaker. He had traveled to New Delhi to attend the funeral of Nehru, but only months later, in a series of campaign speeches, Bhutto made it clear that any attempts to incorporate Kashmir with India would meet with strong resistance from Pakistan.

The election was a close one—Ayub had been accused of corruption and mismanagement—but the emotional plea signaling that Pakistan would still stay strong on the Kashmir issue met with support in many areas, particularly rural communities and those closer to the Kashmir border. For Ayub, it was a costly victory. Many of his accomplishments in shaping a more coherent government for Pakistan were lost in the last-minute campaigning by Bhutto. Rather than being able to focus on additional plans for domestic progress, Ayub found himself entering a new term in his presidency saddled with the responsibility of living up to the promises Bhutto had made—to resolve the Kashmir conflict, and do it quickly.

Disputes over the province of Kashmir have kept India and Pakistan in conflict for decades. As Foreign Minister, Zulfikar Ali Bhutto encouraged a quick solution—sparking a series of armed conflicts.

In March and April of 1965, with tensions high along the border, Indian and Pakistani troops engaged in a small skirmish in a swampy, relatively barren border region near the Arabian Sea, known as the Rann of Kutch. The conflict ended with Indian troops retreating. To the Pakistani army, this retreat, plus India's recent defeat in a 1962 border war with China, led to a sense of confidence that they were operating from a position of strength. President Ayub was busily constructing a new government, but Bhutto was quick to step into the void. As Foreign Minister, Bhutto spent much of his time meeting with army officers to discuss the strengths and weaknesses of the Indian and Pakistani armies.

The death of Nehru had led to similar posturing on the Indian side of the border. Nehru's successor, Prime Minister Shastri, was anxious to prove that he was no weak substitute. Shastri was not eager to fight, but his words did not accurately mirror his personal desire for a peaceful solution.

Tensions escalated. Ayub, as a former military man, was more aware than Bhutto of the weaknesses of the Pakistani army, and he was not so willing to spark a war. He opened up diplomatic negotiations to decide the fate of the Rann of Kutch, hoping not only to prevent the conflict from growing there but also to prevent it from spreading to Kashmir or East Pakistan. The rearrest of Sheikh Abdulla—the Kashmiri leader—and India's strong response to demonstrations in Kashmir did little to cool the temperature.

By the summer of 1965, calls for assistance to the Kashmiri demonstrators were growing. The military fanned the flames, clearly believing that their forces were superior to the Indian army. Bhutto and others made it clear, in a series of governmental meetings, that the time to strike was while Pakistan could still operate from a so-called position of superiority. India was shaping its new government, and because of this was relatively unprepared for war. But it would not stay unprepared for long. Its alliances with the U.S. and Soviet Union would quickly provide it with a ready source of arms. It was clear that Pakistan must strike immediately, while it was still confident of victory.

On July 28, 1965, a small group of Pakistani commandos launched "Operation Gibraltar." The raid was intended to be a secret operation against the Indian-held region of Kashmir, but it quickly collapsed. The commandos were forced to retreat in the face of a fierce counterattack by Indian forces, and more Indian reinforcements quickly arrived as news of the raid reached Indian command. Pakistan had hoped the Kashmiri "freedom fighters" would rally to assist the Pakistani insurgents, but instead the Kashmiri leaders were quickly arrested, preventing them from mounting any kind of resistance. Pakistan's plans for a surprise raid, and for the solid support of local Kashmiris, were quickly eliminated. Operation Gibraltor was a failure.

But the Pakistani army was not finished. A decision was made—whether authorized by Bhutto or Ayub is not clear—to escalate the fighting with "Operation Grand Slam." Operation Grand Slam involved plans to send the Pakistani army across the border into Indian territory—territory that was not part of the disputed region of Kashmir. It was clear that this action would launch a full-scale war with India, and yet the Pakistan army was given the go-ahead.

Operation Grand Slam began on August 30, 1965. It ended three days later, as Indian forces fiercely fought back and contained any effort by the Pakistani army to penetrate Indian territory. With the failure of the mission, Ayub clearly needed to call for a retreat. But before he could do so, Indian troops launched their own attack, this time all along the West Pakistan frontier, centering on the city of Lahore. The Pakistani army had launched a minor skirmish, confident of victory, and instead found itself losing a far-larger war.

As the Indian army advanced along the border, two efforts by India to negotiate peace were ignored by the Pakistani government. Both sides, because of, or in spite of, the posturing of their leaders, found themselves locked in a war. But international pressure soon took the decisionmaking from their hands. The U.N. Secretary General, U Thant, flew to Pakistan to try to arrange a

In September of 1965, U.S. President Lyndon Johnson used an arms embargo against both India and Pakistan to force a cease-fire. Short on resources, and unable to find help from other Islamic nations, Pakistan was forced to lay down its guns.

cease-fire. The United States brought its own pressure to bear. President Lyndon Johnson ordered an embargo on any sales of arms to either India or Pakistan. For India, this was a relatively small problem—the Soviet Union was happy to supply arms to fill the gap. But for Pakistan, heavily dependent on the United States for its weapons and military supplies, the embargo was a disaster. Pakistan, which had felt so confident of its military superiority only a short time ago, now found itself in a nightmarish situation—fighting a war on three fronts (Kashmir, along the West Pakistan border, and defending East Pakistan) without the supplies it needed to keep fighting.

Pakistan turned now to other Muslim countries for support, but they too refused. By September 15, Pakistan's supplies were almost gone—there were no spare parts or fuel for aircraft, no ammunition for the troops. A cease-fire was finally brokered by the Soviet Union on September 22. Only 17 days after the war had begun, Pakistan had suffered a humiliating defeat, tested and found lacking its international alliances, and strengthened the position of India's new prime minister.

Ayub traveled to the Soviet Union on January 3, 1966, to meet with Prime Minister Shastri and carve out an agreement to end the hostilities. The meetings were long and fruitless, with neither side willing to agree on the critical point—the fate of Kashmir. After 7 days of tense meetings and under extreme pressure from the international community, in particular their Soviet hosts, Shastri and Ayub finally signed a Soviet-drafted document, known as the Tashkent Agreement. There was little celebration on the Pakistani side. The fate of Kashmir had not been addressed in any kind of specific way. Both sides had barely contained their hostility during the course of the meetings, and the only real achievement was an agreement to end the fighting.

Ayub knew that he would be returning to a public-relations nightmare. The Pakistani people had been subjected to intense media propaganda, boasting of Pakistan's success in the fighting and of how the Indian forces had been routinely beaten back from the border and defeated. The Tashkent Agreement would soon make it clear that the truth was quite different from what had been reported. At least, Ayub hoped, he would be able to work with Shastri to progress from the sketchy outlines spelled out in the agreement to something more concrete—a resolution to the Kashmir situation.

But even this small hope would be dashed. India's Prime Minister Shastri suffered a heart attack and died the night before both sides were to leave the Soviet Union. Ayub helped to carry the prime minister's body to the airplane that would carry it back to India. Then he too left the Soviet Union. There were no clear answers about what the future held for India and Pakistan.

4

A Nation Undivided

The war in Kashmir had been witnessed first-hand by Nehru's daughter, Indira Gandhi. She had been in the Kashmiri capital, Srinagar, planning a restful vacation in the beautiful city. But shortly before she arrived, Operation Gibraltor had been launched. When her plane landed, she was informed that Pakistani troops had crossed the border, and it was suggested that she should return to India at once. She refused, and instead went immediately to a military command post in the city where she phoned Prime Minister Shastri and informed him of the conflict. She knew that this was no skirmish—she sensed that Pakistan would use this minor incursion as the starting point for a much larger battle. She was correct.

By the time Indira left Kashmir, she had played an integral role in the early stages of the conflict. It was her first opportunity to play a leadership role in the India/Pakistan conflict. It would not be her last.

Indira Gandhi was born on November 19, 1917, the first

Daughter of Prime Minister Nehru, Indira Gandhi soon found herself thrust into the political spotlight. In January 1966, Indira Gandhi was sworn in as India's third prime minister.

child of a man who would soon embark on a pivotal political career. The fight for the cause of independence marked her early life—her father and grandfather were frequently imprisoned for their views, and her mother was also deeply involved in the fight for freedom. Her earliest memory is of her family gathering together to burn foreign cloth and all imported goods in the court-yard of the family's home. From the age of three she, like the rest of her family, would wear cloth that had been spun by hand, called *khadi*.

By the time she was 11, Indira had become directly involved in the independence movement. She was part of the "Monkey Brigade," an organization of children whose job it was to warn members of the Congress Party and others involved in the peaceful resistance movement that British soldiers were about to arrest them. The message would arrive from an informer and Indira and other children would race to the home of the target, warning him or her that soldiers were on their way. By the time the soldiers arrived, their target had vanished.

At the age of 24, Indira married Feroze Gandhi. Despite sharing the same last name, her husband was not related to Mohandas Gandhi. In fact, her father strongly objected to Indira's marriage to Feroze, on the grounds that he was much poorer and of a different faith (Indira was Hindu, Feroze was Parsi) than she was. Also, by this point Nehru was relying heavily on Indira, especially following the death of her mother. But the marriage proceeded, with a honeymoon spent in Kashmir.

When Nehru became prime minister, Indira and Feroze moved into the official residence with him. The family had now grown to include two sons, Rajiv and Sanjay, and Indira divided most of her time between assisting her father and supervising her sons. Her husband began to focus on his own political career, and soon they grew apart and decided to separate. Feroze would die of a heart attack at the age of 48.

Indira became increasingly involved in her father's official business, frequently serving as a hostess to important political guests and organizing state dinners and other formal occasions. Her prominent position brought her into contact with important politicians, and it was not long before she was persuaded to become more directly involved in politics. In 1955 she was nominated for membership on the Congress Working Committee, a significant spot in the dominant political party, and one that brought her more clearly into the public eye. By 1959, she was elected president of the Congress party—a position that both her grandfather and father had once held. She served for only one year, but played a "behind the scenes" role in advising her father in the final years of his life.

Following Nehru's death, Indira somewhat reluctantly joined his successor's cabinet as minister for information and broadcasting. It was a fairly small cabinet position, and Indira was not terribly fond of the media, but it would mark a turning point in her political career. She began to follow a habit her father had had as prime minister—from 8:00 to 9:00 A.M. every morning she held a kind of "open house," in which people of all walks of life were invited to come to see her, share their complaints and discuss their concerns. She also traveled extensively throughout India, holding meetings with workers and leaders, obtaining a new respect and prominence as a politician in her own right, rather than simply as Nehru's daughter. It is likely that she was already laying the groundwork for a future campaign for prime minister.

When news of Shastri's death reached her, Indira held a

meeting with several of her key advisers. She was interested in becoming prime minister, but knew that any obvious campaigning for the job would seem awkward. Through skillful maneuvering, she was able to ensure that her name was quietly put forward by others.

On January 19, 1966, the 526 Congress members of Parliament gathered to elect their next leader. During the nearly four hours of voting, crowds gathered outside the Central Hall to learn who would be the next leader. Finally, a Congress Party representative came outside and shouted, "It's a girl!" Five days later, Indira was sworn in as India's third prime minister.

The country she now was charged with leading did not present her with an easy job. Two recent wars (with China and Pakistan) and two new leaders in four years had created a climate of uncertainty. The monsoons (yearly rains) had failed for two years, leaving parts of the country grappling with famine. The border areas were still sites of unrest. The economy was wrestling with inflation.

Her early days as prime minister were a struggle. She was not a strong public speaker, and not able to think quickly. With domestic policies nearing crisis status, Indira planned a trip to the United States in an effort to win additional United States aid for the famine-stricken country as well as to bolster her leadership position. The trip was a tremendous success, and Indira took advantage of an opportunity to address the United Nations to make it clear that India would not concede on the issue of Kashmir. Stressing that Kashmir was a vital strategic asset to India in light of the recent hostilities with China, she stated, "We cannot and will not tolerate a second partition of India on religious grounds. It would destroy the very basis of the Indian state." Her strong words still echo today in those who explain the essence of India's position on Kashmir.

In her early days as prime minister, Indira Gandhi negotiated with U.S. President Johnson to provide aid to India's famine-stricken people. She later used the relationship to strengthen India's commitment to retaining the province of Kashmir.

A NEW PARTITION

Indira would soon be forced to take a position on yet another disputed region—the territory known as Punjab. Located just south of Kashmir in the northern section of India, Punjab is strategically significant for its location (India's capital of Delhi lies along its eastern border; along its western border is Pakistan) and for its agricultural riches, particularly wheat. But the region had been polarized since before independence, marked by often violent conflict between Hindus and Sikhs. When it became clear that Muslims would be granted their own state, the Sikhs quickly protested for their own region, based in Punjab. But their claims were denied.

By the time Indira became Prime Minister, the Sikh agitations had gone on for many years. They fought bravely and fiercely in the Indian army during the wars with Pakistan, but then returned to protest for their rights to have their own independent state. Indira decided to resolve the Sikh problem by giving them their own region, but only in a portion of Punjab, not the whole territory. On November 1, 1966, India was once more divided—and a new state, to become known as Khalistan, was created.

It was a controversial decision. Many felt that the Sikhs deserved their own state as a way of thanking them for their critical role in the Indian-Pakistan wars. Others felt that the Sikh population would soon not be satisfied merely with their own state within India, but would demand that this state become independent. They would be proved correct.

Indira emphasized that she had no intention of allowing religion to divide India, though it might carve out a state within India. Her father had intended that India would be a secular (non-religious) state from its independence, and she underlined this in her choice of President for India in the 1967 elections. She selected Zakir Husain, a Muslim. It was, of course, a controversial choice, and one opposed by many in the Congress Party. Indira's choice prevailed, however, and Husain was elected. He would serve only until May 3, 1969, when he died of a heart attack, but his brief tenure as president proved that there was a place for Muslims in Indian politics—the vindication of the position Nehru had taken before Pakistan was created.

And yet Hindu-Muslim conflict still lingered, just below the surface, waiting for a spark to ignite it yet again. That spark would bring India and Pakistan to war once again, this time in East Pakistan.

WAR FOR INDEPENDENCE

While Indira Gandhi was building a political power base in India, Pakistan had been stricken with political chaos. Pakistan's Prime Minister Ayub had, as expected, returned from Moscow to face a public outraged by the embarrassing end to the war. Ayub became ill with pneumonia, and during his illness control of the country was assumed (some critics said seized) by General Agha Muhammad Yahya Khan. Ayub ultimately did return to work, but he had grown weaker during his sickness and the general and his military had grown stronger. Public unrest dominated the streets of Pakistan, riots were common, and Ayub was forced to rely more and more heavily on the military to maintain order and keep the peace.

Many of the protests centered on a dissatisfaction with the political system in place. The thousand miles separating East and West Pakistan seemed to have grown wider in recent years. Representatives from West Pakistan traditionally dominated the government, leaving those in East Pakistan disturbed at their inability to help shape national decisions. The conflict was more subtle than simply between East and West Pakistan; it also centered around ethnic groups—the Punjabis from West Pakistan seemed to dominate the government both nationally and even within East Pakistan itself, where many important government positions were held by Punjabis, rather than the Bengalis that made up the majority of East Pakistan's population. The question of language still rankled, as well, among Bengalis forced to speak Urdu, the "official" language of Pakistan.

As the country lurched toward civil war, General Yahya placed greater and greater pressure on Prime Minister Ayub to step down. Finally, on March 25, 1969, he agreed, publicly announcing his decision to pass all authority to General Yahya. The clock quickly turned backward in Pakistan. Once more, martial law was declared, political parties were banned and the constitution (created in 1962) was considered no longer valid. Ayub's cabinet members were fired, as were all the governors of Pakistan's provinces.

PARTITION OF PAKISTAN

For more than a year, martial law prevailed in Pakistan. Protestors were violently suppressed. Yahya was confident enough of the changes martial law had brought about to call for new elections to be held in December of 1970. But the results were quite different from what he had expected. A majority of the legislative seats in Pakistan's National Assembly were won by members of the Awami League, the leading political party in East Pakistan, led by Sheikh Mujibur Rahman. Sheikh Rahman immediately let Yahya know that, as the leader of the majority party, he expected to be named prime minister—a position to which he should have been entitled based on his party's winning of the majority of all votes. In addition, he requested an immediate change in army policy, to ensure that more Bengalis were given military positions.

But this was not the end to Yahya's electoral problems. A new party—the Pakistan People's Party (PPP)—had been founded by Ayub's former foreign minister, Zulfikar Bhutto. The PPP had won the majority of votes in West Pakistan,

After the resignation of Pakistani Prime Minister Ayub in 1969, control of the country fell to General Yahya Khan, a hard-liner who banned political parties, declared martial law, and removed all provincial governors.

based largely on Bhutto's campaign promises of an end to military and religious tyranny.

Caught between two unpleasant options, Yahya chose the less problematic. He formed an alliance with Bhutto. As a result of this behind-the-scenes dealmaking, Bhutto made it clear (just before the National Assembly was scheduled to open) that he and his party would not participate in the Assembly until he could meet with Sheikh Rahman to discuss the best ways to proceed with governing Pakistan. With this handy excuse, Yahya announced that the opening of the National Assembly would be indefinitely postponed until the conflict between the two leading parties could be resolved.

The fate of Pakistan rested, in a sense, in the hands of ambitious men who put their own pursuit of personal power well above the needs of a country in crisis. Had Bhutto and Rahman been able to cooperate, had Yahya been willing to recognize the people's wishes in the election results, war might have been avoided. But they were not.

East Pakistan immediately erupted in protests—protests that were brutally put down by the military. Bengali protestors were particularly targeted; Bengali women were frequently subjected to violence at the hands of Punjabi soldiers. And so civil war came to Pakistan, as East Pakistan's hopes for a greater voice in the national government were once more dashed. All Bengalis quickly rallied together, united as never before against the violent oppression at the hands of the military. They were no longer interested in a greater role in Pakistan's government. They now wanted a government of their own. The requests for greater autonomy had changed into cries for independence.

In March of 1971, the contrast between India and Pakistan could not have been greater. As Indira Gandhi celebrated the validation of her policies in successes in the general election and set about forming her new government, the leader of Pakistan, General Yahya, ordered a complete military crackdown in East Pakistan. As images of the violence filtered out through the international media, criticism of the Pakistani regime was immediate and harsh.

A harsh ruler, General Yahya Khan cracked down on Hindus in East Pakistan. He answered cries for an independent state of Bangladesh with a series of arrests and executions.

And still the crackdown continued. The army's net of targets widened to include all Hindus in East Pakistan, as rumor spread that many of these Hindus were really Indian spies, sent to East Pakistan to encourage the troubles and advance India's interests. The conflict did begin to affect India, as thousands of Bengali refugees fled East Pakistan and poured into the Indian region of West Bengal.

Indian officials quickly made it clear to Pakistan that they must allow these refugees to return to their own homes, as India was ill prepared to handle a refugee population that threatened to grow to millions. When there was little satisfactory response from the Pakistani government, it became clear that Pakistan's civil war threatened to affect the entire subcontinent.

Indira Gandhi agreed to allow the Awami League to set up a government-in-exile in the Indian city of Calcutta. As early as April of 1971, Indira Gandhi began to discuss with her senior officials the preparations that would be needed for a war with Pakistan.

But the first steps were small ones. India began to assist the Bengali independence movement, providing the freedom fighters with training and weapons. While the actions were taken in part out of sympathy for the terrible situation the people of East Pakistan were in, they did little to end the massacres of Hindus in the region. It was becoming clear that the government of Pakistan was systematically murdering and driving out its own citizens.

India pressured the international community to become involved in solving the crisis. By now, the number of refugees in India had risen to several million, and their care was creating an economic crisis. In a series of speeches, Indira Gandhi began referring to the stricken region as Bangladesh—the name the Bengali independence movement had chosen—rather than East Pakistan. Diplomats exchanged heated words, but little action was taken. The matter was judged by many to be an internal matter involving disputes between different groups of Pakistanis. Indeed, much of the international community's leaders supported Pakistan in its efforts to maintain order within its own borders.

But Indira Gandhi did not believe that it was simply

a matter of maintaining the peace. In her view, the people of East Pakistan had spoken—in a legal election—and their voices and wishes had been ignored by their own government.

WAR AND PEACE

In November of 1971, units based on either side of the East Pakistan frontier engaged in early skirmishes, as more Indian Army units were moved to the border to provide reinforcements. The Pakistan senior military command ignored these warning signs, believing they were merely border skirmishes intended to put pressure on diplomatic negotiations rather than the early stages of a major military campaign.

They were wrong. Indira Gandhi, under the advice of her military leaders, had authorized a major offensive designed to completely overwhelm the Pakistan Army, drive Pakistan forces out of East Bengal, and oversee the creation of an independent nation to be known as Bangladesh. It is certain that this invasion of a neighboring country would have been harshly criticized by the international community. But only days before the Indian Army offensive was scheduled to begin, the Pakistani air force attacked eight Indian military bases, inside Indian territory. India responded by quickly declaring war—a war that could now be justified as a response to an unjustified attack on Indian soil.

The Pakistani air attack was a serious miscalculation on General Yahya's part. He had counted on his allies, China and the United States, to step in, as they had been critical of India's posturing on the issue of Bangladesh during private and public diplomatic meetings. But the fact that Pakistan attacked first ruined any diplomatic claims that India was

After the 1971 attacks on India failed miserably, Pakistan was forced to concede on the issue of Bangladesh's independence. Here, citizens of Bangladesh display their flag. Shortly afterward, General Yahya Khan resigned as Pakistan's president, and was replaced by former Foreign Minister Bhutto.

interfering in a neighboring nation's internal policies.

The Pakistan Army was almost immediately over-whelmed. India's forces were superior. The Pakistani military had been fighting a number of battles in their efforts to maintain the peace and eliminate terrorist activities—they were now spread all over the country and were unable to quickly organize a unified fighting force to beat back the

Indian Army. And India did not confine its targets to Bangladesh. Having quickly penetrated the western border of East Pakistan, the army moved beyond the goal of supporting the creation of Bangladesh to eliminating Pakistan's ability to start any future conflicts. Indian forces pushed into Western Pakistan and into Pakistani-held parts of Kashmir.

The PPP candidate Zulfikar Bhutto was called into action. General Yahya had appointed him Deputy Prime Minister just before the war began, and only a few days later he was sent to New York to meet with representatives from the U.S. and U.N. It was made clear to Bhutto by the U.S. that there was only one way to save Pakistan at this point, and that was to give part of it up.

Pakistan formally surrendered on December 16, 1971, having suffered a humiliating defeat in a war that had lasted only 11 days. Nearly 100,000 Pakistani soldiers were seized and held as prisoners of war. The exact number of Pakistani soldiers killed in the war is not known, but many reports describe the path of the Indian invasion as being littered with acres of dead Pakistani soldiers. General Yahya was forced to step down in disgrace. Bhutto would succeed him in administering the shattered remains of Pakistan. It was a time of joy and celebration in India, but in Pakistan there were few cheers when Bhutto became Pakistan's president on December 20. The military regime had ended, but half of the country had been lost.

5

The Pursuit of Power

In the 1970s, the fate of Pakistan rested in the hands of its new leader, Zulfikar Bhutto. Previous administrations had ended in disgrace, the country had been divided by civil war, and the army had been humiliated by the quick defeat by Indian forces. Bhutto did not waste time. He quickly consolidated his own power by keeping martial law in force throughout the country, but giving himself (rather than the military) the responsibility for enforcing it.

It was during his time as Pakistan's leader that Islamic values became a more important part of Pakistan's political life. But Bhutto was not interested in creating a strict Islamic state. Instead, his ideal was a blend of Islamic tradition with socialist principles. It was a plan that called for the people of Pakistan to put the common good above the interests of individuals—the notable exception to this being, of course, Bhutto himself. The state he was shaping was one in which he ruled, supreme and unchallenged. Any political friends or foes who dared to question his leadership might find

Although he ruled on domestic issues with an iron hand, Pakistani President Bhutto knew the value of diplomacy. In this 1974 photo, Bhutto (right) greets Syrian President Hafez al-Assad (center) at the Lahore airport.

themselves immediately out of a job—or worse.

But while Bhutto ruled domestic issues with an iron hand, he was not oblivious to Pakistan's critical need to build international alliances through skillful diplomacy. Within one year of becoming the leader of Pakistan, Bhutto began diplomatic negotiations with Indira Gandhi. By July 1972, these had led to a face-to-face meeting between the two leaders at the Indian resort of Simla. While neither side particularly trusted the other, and they initially disagreed on several important issues— Pakistan wanted India to hold a vote in Kashmir, allowing its people to determine their status; India wanted Pakistan to officially recognize the new nation of Bangladesh—they ultimately carved out the Simla Agreement. It spelled out terms for an end to border disputes, and promised future progress on the status of Kashmir, but the recognition of Bangladesh and the exchange of prisoners of war would take another year or more before they were finally addressed. While the Simla Agreement laid the groundwork for future cooperation, India and Pakistan would not fully renew their diplomatic relations for another four years.

NEIGHBORING DICTATORSHIPS

For many years, the clearest difference between Pakistan and India was that Pakistan had most recently been governed under martial law by one absolute ruler, while India has operated as a democracy. In June 1975, that changed. Indira Ghandi was charged with election fraud—her crime centered around the illegal use of a government official in her reelection efforts, as well as the illegal use of government funds to rent loudspeakers and other equipment for a campaign rally.

These were relatively minor offences, but under India's strict laws governing political campaigns, they were enough to prevent an official from holding elected office for six years. Indira Gandhi would need to step down as prime minister.

Her political opponents were quick to capitalize on the situation. India's economy was suffering, in part from the cost of assimilating so many refugees from Bangladesh. The war, while successful, had also been expensive. And there were many who disagreed with Indira's policies. They were all quick to call for her immediate resignation.

But Indira had quite a different plan in mind. With the assistance of India's president, her close ally, India was immediately placed under a "state of emergency," under the official explanation that plots against the prime minister were threatening to completely destabilize India. All of her critics were immediately arrested. Newspapers and media outlets were closed. Next to be placed in prison were lawyers and journalists, as well as student protestors—in short, anyone who might question the steps she was taking. Opposition political parties were banned. Foreign media was censored. In all, more than 75,000 people were put in prison as a result of Indira's actions.

For the rest of her term as prime minister (21 months), Indira functioned as a kind of dictator, arresting anyone who opposed her and shaping India's policies purely on her own authority. And when she finally called for democratic elections again, in 1977, she was soundly defeated. Most Indians had supported Indira, but they would not accept the absolute control of any leader.

Indira would spend three years out of office before being reelected prime minister in 1980. During that time, she

After the failure of increasingly harsh policies that attempted to silence critics and consolidate power, Indira Gandhi was voted out of office in 1977. She returned, however, three years later, reaffirming her commitment to a more representative, less authoritarian government.

made it clear that she had received the message voters sent to her. She traveled throughout the Indian countryside, visiting people and showing them that she shared their concerns. She would be reelected. India had not rejected her; they had rejected a totalitarian form of government.

BHUTTO IN CHARGE

In Pakistan, no swift denial of authoritarian regimes was taking place. Bhutto was firmly in charge—he extended his reach by dismissing regional governors who were protesting, publicly or privately, against his policies and replacing them with his own party loyalists. It was in Pakistan's remote regions that trouble continued to come, and even as the civil war faded into a memory, the country still struggled with the difficulty of unifying so many different groups into a single nation.

It was and is one of the greatest difficulties hampering Pakistan's efforts to become a strong and successful country. A nation, artificially shaped from the very beginning, from lines drawn on a map and later as a result of war, may find that its center is weaker than its separate parts, and this has been Pakistan's fate. Its people often feel greater loyalty to their own regions than to their country as a whole. They are more likely to identify themselves by their ethnic heritage or the territory they are from, rather than as Pakistanis.

Bhutto attempted to address this problem by firmly dominating and controlling the regional governors. He also turned his sights to the global community, attempting to build alliances to create an identity for Pakistan as part of a larger international group to lead the country beyond its chaotic recent past.

Pakistan had been bitterly disappointed at the Western world's unwillingness to criticize India for its role in the civil war that created Bangladesh from East Pakistan. Bhutto astutely read the anti-western public sentiment, and set about forming alliances with new countries (not coincidentally, countries with authoritative leaders), including China, North Korea and Libya, as well as the

Arab states in the Persian Gulf region and parts of North Africa. He led Pakistan out of the alliances that had previously been strategically important, including the British Commonwealth of National and the Southwest Asia Treaty Organization, but retained relations with Turkey and Iran.

Pakistan also adopted a new constitution in 1973, one that consolidated the powers of the prime minister, but also included an important nod to the conservative Islamic leaders. The constitution stated that no law would be passed that was in conflict with Islamic teaching, that Pakistan was officially an Islamic republic, and that Islam was the state religion.

Bhutto clearly believed that Pakistan's fate was to become the dominant Muslim state. But the rise in international power of certain Persian Gulf States, benefiting from the increasing importance of oil to the world economy, made it clear that the key to international status required more than sheer numbers of people. The global scene was changing. The United States and Russia were negotiating an arms control treaty. Egypt and Israel were meeting to discuss a possible peace agreement. And closer to home, a revolution had happened in Afghanistan, while India had been transformed from a democracy into a dictatorship. It was clear that there was a new world order developing. And Bhutto wanted Pakistan to be at the top.

The path to power became clear in May of 1974, when India detonated a nuclear device in Rajasthan. India claimed that the test was carried out for "peaceful, civilian purposes," and certainly it had a domestic benefit—signaling to the Indian people that their homeland had entered the select group of nations that were nuclear powers. Indira Gandhi certainly understood that the explosion would cause panic in Pakistan. On May 22, four days after the explosion, she

The 1974 detonation of a nuclear bomb in the desert near New Delhi brought sharp criticism from Pakistan. Since then, nuclear escalation on both sides has brought increased fear and strain to India-Pakistan relations.

wrote a letter to Bhutto, saying, "We in India have condemned and will continue to condemn military uses of nuclear energy as a threat to humanity. . . . There are no political or foreign policy implications of this test."

Bhutto was not reassured. The test had provided an excuse to explore a new route to pushing Pakistan into a more powerful international position. Bhutto determined that Pakistan would also become a member of the nuclear powers, this time as the only Islamic nation to possess a nuclear weapon.

ARMS AND ALLAH

The reaction to India's nuclear test was immediate and critical. Concern about the spread of nuclear weapons technology prompted the international community to put pressure on India to halt its nuclear technology program and to prevent Pakistan from developing its own.

By the late 1970s, Indira Gandhi was out of power. India, for the first time in its history, was being led by a Prime Minister who was not from the Congress party—Moraji Desai. Desai was suspicious of nuclear technology and, following his public speeches expressing misgivings about the safety of the program, India's arms development program shifted away from nuclear weaponry during the several years he was prime minister.

Pakistan, too, was facing a change in leadership. Pakistan held elections in March of 1977. Bhutto won a resounding victory, due in part to various maneuvers that ensured that he and other PPP members ran unopposed in their respective districts. But while Bhutto stood alone on the ballot, he was facing a formidable opponent through-out the campaign. Islamic fundamentalists had had enough of Bhutto's lifestyle and lukewarm support of

Islamic values. And under the Constitution of 1973, Islam had become a significant force in Pakistani politics. It was not to be treated lightly.

To no one's surprise, Bhutto won the election, but the Islamic fundamentalist groups were not put down as quickly as Bhutto had hoped. They had many supporters within the armed forces. Fearing the worst, Bhutto made a half-hearted attempt to demonstrate his devotion to Islam, closing bars and movie theaters and making the consumption of alcohol illegal, but it was too little too late. Early on the morning of July 5, 1977, Bhutto had a visitor. General Zia Haq, commander of the Pakistan Army, informed him that he was out of a job. He was taken into "protective custody" and martial law was declared. Pakistan was, once more, in the hands of its military.

General Zia was part of the group within the military that devotedly supported Islamic fundamentalism. They believed that Pakistan's troubles stemmed from the lack of a unifying force, and that Islam could be the glue that cemented the country together.

After three weeks, Bhutto was released from custody and allowed to return home, where he was greeted by welcoming crowds. The enthusiasm for Bhutto alarmed General Zia and his colleagues, who had no wish to see their new government overthrown by a sudden surge of popular support for the former leader. After only a few weeks of freedom, Bhutto was once more seized and imprisoned, this time officially charged with a variety of serious crimes including murder—a claim that he had arranged for the death of a political opponent. A quick trial found him guilty, and the former prime minister was sentenced to death. On April 4, 1979, he was hanged, and then quickly buried. His wife and daughter, Benazir, under house arrest, were not permitted to attend the burial.

After the execution of Pakistani leader Zulfikar Ali Bhutto, Pakistan moved toward Islamic fundamentalism. Under President Zia Ul-Haq (seen here in 1986), all civil law was made subject to the traditional teachings of Islam.

The Islamization of Pakistan began in a complete and systematic way following the execution of Bhutto. The memories of the beloved founder, Jinnah, appearing often in public with his unveiled sister (who played a political role in Pakistan's early days) had faded. Pakistan had now become more than a country for Muslims—it was a totally Muslim country. Islamic courts were set up—Pakistan was to be governed in strict accordance with Islamic rules and traditions. *Shari'a* (Islamic law) was made supreme—all civil law was made subject to the traditional teachings of Islam.

It was a time of confusion in the region. Indira Gandhi had returned to power in India in January of 1980. A fundamentalist Islamic movement had overthrown the monarch of Iran. In Afghanistan, Soviet forces had invaded. In light of the instability in much of the region, the United States searched for allies and found them in Pakistan's leadership. Overlooking the somewhat questionable circumstances of Zia's elevation to power, the United States was willing to supply Pakistan with aid and even weapons.

CHILDREN OF POWER

In October of 1984, Indira Gandhi made a series of political speeches designed to address growing concerns about national security and domestic unrest. She had opened a new military school, where students would be trained in the construction and operation of guided missiles. She spoke about the external and internal threats to India's stability.

India was facing new signs of unrest, this time from Sikh terrorists who were, once more, agitating for their own separate state in Punjab. There were more than 14 million Sikhs living in India, most of them moderates who were not in favor of the militants' terrorist tactics. But then the climate changed. In June of 1984, a group of Sikh terrorists seized the holy Golden Temple in Amritsar, at a time when thousands of men, women and children were participating in a pilgrimage to the holy site. The Indian Army had stormed the temple and captured the terrorists, but as a result of the violent exchange of gunfire between terrorists and the army, thousands of innocent people were killed in the crossfire. India's Sikh population was horrified at the loss of life and the extensive damage done to their Golden Temple.

On the morning of October 31, Indira Gandhi was leaving her home to walk to her first appointment of the day. As she crossed the lawn and headed toward her office, a member of her security guard stepped forward. He was a 28-year-old former policeman who had served the prime minister for six years. He was also a Sikh.

The security guard pulled out a gun, pointed it at the Prime Minister, and fired three times. As her body fell to the ground, another Sikh security guard jumped out from a hedge and began to shoot at the leader with an automatic rifle, firing 29 bullets in rapid sequence. She died instantly.

At the time of her death, Indira's 40-year-old son, Rajiv, was traveling through West Bengal. It was part of his political education, a plan at broadening his political experience so that, one day, he might be prepared to follow in his mother's footsteps. That day would come sooner than had been expected. Nine hours after his mother's death, Rajiv Gandhi was sworn in as the new prime minister.

The news of Indira's assassination sparked a wave of anti-Sikh violence. For five days, rampaging mobs targeted Sikh communities, particularly in Delhi. Thousands died in the violence, and millions of dollars of property was destroyed.

And in Pakistan, another leader's child was in the process of recreating a dynasty. Benazir Bhutto, the daughter of the assassinated Pakistani leader, had set about organizing her own resistance movement to the military regime of General Zia, first in exile in London and then later in her own homeland. She was forced out of her country after being arrested for violating the martial law regulations against organizing demonstrations against the government, but the dynamic young woman quickly became an international celebrity. It seemed increasingly likely that she would avenge her father through her own political triumphs.

But General Zia would meet his end not through political campaigns but through violence. On August 17, 1988, Zia traveled to a site near Bahawalpur, where a test of military equipment had brought together the Pakistani leader plus the American Ambassador and a U.S. Brigadier General. Accompanied by 28 Pakistani military officers, this elite group boarded a plane heading back to the capital. They never arrived. Their plane crashed shortly after take-off. While equipment failure was the official cause, it was later learned that the equipment had failed as a result of sabotage.

In November 1988, elections were held in Pakistan. Benazir Bhutto, now leader of the PPP, formed alliances with a number of smaller political parties, and it was this coalition government that ruled Pakistan. Benazir Bhutto, a 36-year-old woman, became the prime minister of a Muslim nation, the same nation that had sentenced her father to death.

It would be a difficult assignment. The power of Islamic fundamentalists had increased in recent years, and there were few supporters for the new female prime minister among them. She had cultivated strong alliances with the west and these had served her well during exile, but were a political liability when she took office. She was able to coordinate the successful delivery of weapons from the United States, but part of the price tag was her agreement to slow down Pakistan's nuclear weapons development.

And she soon was confronted with the same problems

Following the 1988 death of President Zia at the hands of saboteurs, elections were again held in Pakistan. Benazir Bhutto, daughter of executed leader Zulfikar Ali Bhutto, forged the alliances needed to secure her place as prime minister. Here she is seen on a diplomatic visit to Iran in 1995.

that had plagued Pakistan for years: the difficulty of building a strong central government in the face of opposition from powerful regional governors, and growing signs of conflict with India—once more in Kashmir.

INDIA ON THE BRINK

In the eyes of many, Rajiv Gandhi had been unprepared when public tragedy and personal ambition thrust him into the role of Prime Minister. Lacking the time to thoughtfully develop his own plans and policies for India's development, he was left to cobble together programs based on his mother's programs, the advice of political colleagues, and his own leanings. The greatest impact of his tenure as prime minister lies in India's technological development. Rajiv was interested in the impact of technology on the military, and so following Rajiv's swearing-in, a plan to modernize the military through increased reliance on technology was launched.

In 1987, these efforts to beef up the military almost pushed India and Pakistan into another war. A peacetime military exercise, known as "Operation Brasstacks," was incorrectly interpreted by Pakistani officials as the prelude to a military campaign. The confusion and mistaken signals were eventually clarified, but the willingness of both sides to misinterpret events made it clear that there was not yet peace between these two neighbors. Indian officials believed that Pakistan was secretly supporting the ongoing efforts by terrorists in the Punjab to achieve their separate state. Relations between both Pakistan and India went steadily downhill as the 1980s drew to a close.

The years 1989-90 would bring the end to the administrations of these two children of former leaders. Both governments were charged with corruption; both were ineffective in their efforts to maintain their support; both were unable to resolve the social problems that were increasingly crippling the subcontinent. And both faced strong opposition from religious-based nationalist political parties. In 1989, a group of opposition parties, including the Hindu Bharatiya Janata Party, managed to gather enough votes to throw out Rajiv Gandhi's Congress Party. In August 1990, the Bhutto government was dismissed, and elections held two months later brought political power to the Islamic Democratic Alliance, a coalition of several parties belonging to Pakistan's religious right.

The uncertainty as governments changed hands was mirrored by an increase in tensions in Kashmir. There had been an upswing in rebel activity in the region in December of 1989. India clearly felt that Pakistan was responsible. The Line of Control—the loose border that had been put in place years earlier to mark the end of the last war—was unsuccessful in stopping the flow of rebels into Kashmir.

India began to make plans for war, examining the various possibilities for attacking across the border. It did not take long for the news to reach Pakistan. As the posturing of the two sides increased, the possibility of nuclear war threatened the entire region. International emissaries were sent to plead with both India and Pakistan to stand down, and eventually the tensions eased enough to prevent a war.

Indian and Pakistani politics are often laced with violence, and in 1991 it would claim another victim. On May 27, 1991, campaigning for his party in Tamil Nadu, Rajiv Gandhi was assassinated. He was targeted by extremists from Sri Lanka. With his death, the Nehru/Gandhi political dynasty came to an end. His Congress party would go on to win the national election, but its new prime minister, for the first time in 30 years, would not be a descendant of Nehru.

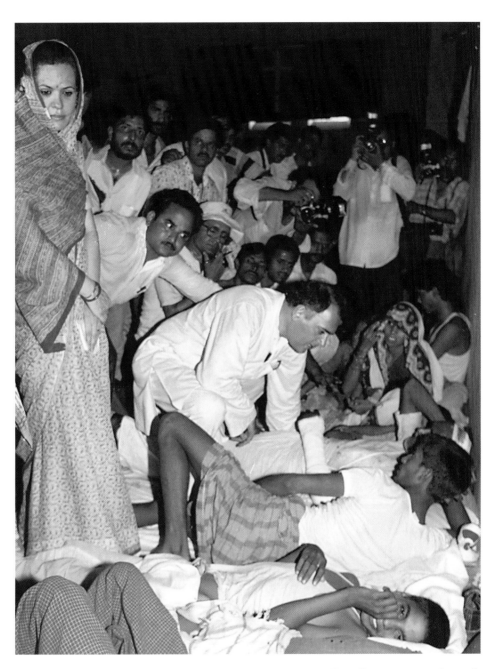

Indira Gandhi's son, Rajiv (center), failed in his attempt to unify India's many peoples and address critical issues of poverty, modernization, and factionalism. His assassination by Sri Lankan extremists ended the era of India's rule by Nehru's descendants.

DIFFERENT ROADS, SAME DESTINATION

In the 1990s, the paths India and Pakistan took were vastly different. Pakistan's Islamic Democratic Alliance had brought Mohammad Nawaz Sharif, the leader of the Pakistan Muslim League, to power. Under Sharif, Pakistan experienced even more widespread Islamization, while Sharif's economic reforms sparked an improved economic picture for the first time in years. But differences with the largest Islamic fundamentalist part of his coalition, the party known as *Jamaat-e-Islami*, and charges of corruption would weaken Sharif's ability to govern. His government was dismissed in April of 1993, reinstated one month later, and then as tensions within the different branches created almost insurmountable problems, Sharif resigned in July.

In October, elections resulted in the PPP coming back to power and with it, once more, Benazir Bhutto became prime minister. But her hold on political power was shaky, based on a serious of alliances with unreliable supporters, and the government would last only three years. In February of 1997, Sharif was back. One of his first political acts was, perhaps not surprisingly, to pass a constitutional amendment making it more difficult for the government in power to be arbitrarily dismissed.

Sharif would return to his former plan, focusing on economic issues in his efforts to oversee increased prosperity for Pakistan. But the center did not hold. Throughout Pakistan's history, its strongest leaders had failed in their efforts to contain regional and religious violence, and the Sharif administration was no exception.

On October 12, 1999, for the fourth time in Pakistan's history, the military led a coup that overthrew the government. General Pervez Musharraf, the head of

Pakistan's armed forces, seized power and declared himself to be the chief executive. It is perhaps an indication of how chaos had become the norm in Pakistan that this sudden ouster of the government inspired little violence, dismay or even concern among the public. In a way, it was business as usual.

Chaos was also rapidly becoming business as usual in India. A series of 10 different governments ruled India in the 1990s, including one (the Hindu-nationalist Bharatiya Janata Party) that held onto power for only 13 days. As the national government struggled with a continuous series of setbacks, it is not surprising that regionally-based political parties became more powerful. Once more, ethnic tensions were on the rise and, yet again, regional issues would begin to dominate national politics.

Pakistan and India had set out on very different paths for modernization in the 1990s. But as the century ended, their paths drew closer. In May of 1998, Pakistan detonated three nuclear devices, a test carried out in response to a similar test carried out by India only two weeks earlier. The conflict had entered a new phase, one threatened by the specter of a nuclear arms race on the subcontinent.

6

The Legacy of Partition

More than half a century has passed since Sir Cyril Radcliffe began the process that would divide India into two. The memories of those still alive who witnessed that time—when India achieved independence and Pakistan became a nation— are tinged with tragedy rather than joy. And, sadly, the legacy of that violent rupture, partitioning the subcontinent along hastily drawn lines, remains one of conflict and violence. The hopes of those who set these events into motion were based on the creation of a peaceful resolution to religious conflicts. But the result has been quite the opposite—two neighboring countries living with decades of festering wounds, each convinced of the rightness of their cause, each armed with nuclear weapons.

The theory of mutual assured destruction—that countries armed with nuclear weapons will be forced to maintain a kind of peace, based on the knowledge that their opponent possesses arms sufficient to kill a significant portion of their population—may prove false here. The conflict between India

The India-Pakistan border remains one of the world's most disputed and dangerous zones—as this sign warns.

and Pakistan is still being written, with each year adding a new page in the saga and a new set of grievances to fuel anger and misunderstanding.

As the 20th century drew to a close, the stage was set for future conflicts. In May 1999, an Indian army patrol discovered the presence of militant insurgents in the

Indian-held portion of northern Kashmir. Fighting broke out in an effort to push back the invading force and reclaim Indian territory. It soon became clear that the militants had received support from Pakistan. In August of that year, a Pakistan naval patrol airplane, officially on a training mission, was shot down by an Indian military plane, resulting in the death of the 16 people on board.

In December of 1999, the conflict was taken to the heart of India. A group of terrorists (Kashmiri separatists) seized an Indian Airlines commercial flight, traveling to New Delhi from Nepal with 189 passengers on board. The hijackers held the plane for eight days, and before the siege had ended, one passenger had been killed.

Conflict continues along the 500-mile Line of Control in Kashmir. Periodic cease-fires, initiated either by India or the pro-Pakistan Kashmiri separatists, have temporarily halted violence in the region, but these have only been short-term stops.

In 2001, President Musharraf and India's Prime Minister, Atal Behari Vajpayee, held a three-day summit in Agra, India. Their goal was to reach a diplomatic and political plan to resolve the crisis in Kashmir, but the summit essentially failed. India feels strongly that Kashmir is an integral part of its homeland, and Pakistani support for the Kashmiri separatists is a violation of India's internal policy. Pakistan feels tied to the largely Muslim population in Kashmir, and insists that India should give the residents the opportunity to vote and essentially choose between remaining part of India or instead separating.

In October 2001, a car bomb was driven into the assembly building in Srinagar, within the India-held portion of Kashmir. The blast killed 40 people. And then, in December 2001, an attack was launched on the Indian

Even as tensions remain high, there are signs of diplomacy. Here Pakistani President General Pervez Musharraf is greeted by Indian Prime Minister Atal Bihari Vajpayee during a visit aimed at resolving the decades-old Kashmir dispute.

Parliament building in New Delhi. Kashmiri militants threw grenades at the building and opened fire. By the time the attack had ended, 14 people were dead.

THE RISE OF FUNDAMENTALISM

The great aims of Jinna and Nehru—to create countries that would be essentially secular, but would provide their people with an opportunity to practice their religion freely—have essentially failed. As time has passed, secularism has vanished from the politics of the subcontinent.

As the 21st century began, India was led by Prime Minister Atal Behari Vajpayee, the founder of the Hindu nationalist Bharatiya Janata Party. Vajpayee is the first Hindu nationalist to become prime minister, but his party's electoral victory is a sign that India is more closely than ever before defining itself as a Hindu nation.

The rise of fundamentalism has a longer history in Pakistani politics. The Islamic fundamentalism movement in Pakistan has been a source of international concern, as more radical elements attempt to use their particular brand of Islamic fundamentalism to draw together disaffected people (generally young men) in a cross-border crusade known as a jihad (holy war). The attack on the United States by representatives of a Muslim fundamentalist group, and the subsequent war launched on their bases in the country of Afghanistan, deeply affected events in India and Pakistan. Pakistan, under General Musharraf's leadership, sided with the United States in its battle against Islamic extremist forces in Afghanistan, a move viewed unfavorably by many Muslims, particularly within his own military. India, in turn, put increasing pressure on Musharraf to combat terrorist elements acting in Kashmir. After the attack on the Indian parliament, the pressure turned to threats of war.

Kashmir has, in a sense, become the visual representation of the conflict that has plagued the subcontinent since Britain's hasty departure in 1947. A region once known principally for its beauty has now become a military staging ground where, in some cases, Pakistani and Indian forces are close enough to see each other, lined up on either side of the Line of Control, waiting for the next conflict. Once the crown jewel in the British Empire, the subcontinent has now become a series of flashpoints, where both sides watch and wait for war to begin. It is a disappointing conclusion to the campaign of non-violence that drew Hindus and Muslims together under the guidance of Mohandas Gandhi.

PROSPECTS FOR PEACE

The long history of conflict in the region makes the prospects for peace dim, at least in the immediate future. It seems unlikely that hostilities, steadily increasing over a period of decades, will be resolved through quick diplomatic intervention.

But there is a critical international element to the prospects for peace in the region. India and Pakistan contain a substantial portion of the world's population. Their strategic importance in global stability became clear during the United States war in Afghanistan. A resolution to the conflict in Southeast Asia will continue to be an international priority in order to maintain an alliance against the spread of additional faith-based terrorist groups.

International pressure will also remain heavy to contain the development of nuclear weapons in the subcontinent. Both sides have expressed their willingness to use their nuclear arsenal, although they officially state that they would not initiate the attack but would use it unhesitatingly in response to an attack from the other side.

The rise of more fundamentalist groups in India and Pakistan is another obstacle to the peace process. The more centrist political parties in both countries have fallen victim to unsuccessful governments and charges of corruption. The staunchly pro-Hindu and pro-Muslim groups that have been the most successful in recent years have won gains largely in their ability to unify diverse people under religious banners. Rather than identifying themselves as Indian or Pakistani, these groups have

In accordance with the terms of the July 2001 summit, Indian prisoners held by Pakistan are allowed to cross the border and return home.

appealed to people who have felt abandoned by their government but have retained strong ties to their religious and ethnic heritage. This sends a frightening message to religious minorities still remaining within the borders of India and Pakistan.

The resolution of the crisis in Kashmir is only one part of the path to peace, but it certainly could prove a critical first step. Kashmir has become the stage on which much of the India-Pakistan conflict has been acted out in recent years. Pakistan's support for separatist groups in Kashmir has only served to increase the likelihood of yet another war in the region. India's unwillingness to allow Kashmiris to decide their own future has only made it more likely that unrest will continue.

The rapid turnover in governments in recent years has added to the climate of instability. There is a sense among the general population that the leadership is temporary, and that a sudden or violent overthrow could happen at any time. Indeed, the people have come to expect it. A government that cannot focus on shaping the future of its country, that must instead focus tremendous energy and resources on stamping out any signs of rebellion and clinging tightly to power, will be unlikely to risk internal discontent by making the concessions necessary to achieve peace.

The hastily drawn borders, drafted by Cyril Radcliffe, were created to prevent war, and yet the wars still came. Mohandas Gandhi sought India's independence with the idea that Hindus, Muslims, and Sikhs could better rule the subcontinent on their own, and yet when the British left, the subcontinent divided and then divided again. Nehru and Jinna dreamed of countries where religious definitions would not matter, and yet their nations have now become countries defined by religion.

Regardless of where the borders may be drawn in the future, it seems sadly certain that the conflict between India and Pakistan will continue.

1947 India gains independence from Britain. Pakistan becomes a nation.

1948 Jinnah dies; India and Pakistan go to war over Kashmir.

1949 Cease-fire in Kashmir. Line of Control drawn where each side occupied territory at the end of fighting.

1962 India goes to war with China.

1954 Nehru dies.

1965 Second war between India and Pakistan over Kashmir.

1966 Indira Gandhi becomes prime minister of India.

1971 East Pakistan attempts to secede; civil war begins. India enters war on behalf of Bengali separatists; Pakistan military surrenders to Indian forces.

1972 Indira Gandhi and Zulfiqar Bhutto sign Simla Agreement, creating new Line of Control.

1974 India tests nuclear device.

1976 India and Pakistan reestablish diplomatic ties.

1979 Islamic penal code introduced into Pakistan law; Bhutto hanged.

1984 Indira Gandhi assassinated.

1988 Benazir Bhutto becomes Pakistan's prime minister, first female prime minister of a Muslim nation.

1990 Coalition of right-wing parties takes power in Pakistan; Sharif becomes prime minister.

1991 Rajiv Gandhi assassinated.

1998 India and Pakistan conduct tests of nuclear devices.

1999 Conflict breaks out between India and Pakistan over Kashmir region; General Musharraf leads military overthrow of Pakistan's government.

2001 Musharraf and Vajpayee meet to discuss Kashmir, but fail to reach agreement; Kashmiri separatists attack Indian parliament.

BOOKS:

Butalia, Urvashi. *The Other Side of Silence: Views from the Partition of India.* Durham, NC: Duke University Press, 2000.

Finck, Lila and Hayes, John P. *Jawaharlal Nehru.* Philadelphia: Chelsea House Publishers, 1987.

Gupte, Pranay. *Mother India: A Political Biography of Indira Gandhi.* New York: Charles Scribner's Sons, 1992.

Harrison, Selig S., Kreisberg, Paul H., and Kux, Dennis (eds.). *India and Pakistan.* Washington, DC: Woodrow Wilson Center Press, 1999.

Read, Anthony and Fisher, David. *The Proudest Day: India's Long Road to Independence.* New York: W.W. Norton & Co., 1997.

Ziring, Lawrence. *Pakistan in the Twentieth Century.* New York: Oxford University Press, 1997.

WEB SITES:

Britannica.com

Frontierpost.com.pk

Kashmirtimes.com

Nic.in

Pak.gov.pk

Pakobserver.com

Timesofindia.com

BOOKS:

Bidwai, Praful and Vanaik, Achin. *New Nukes: India, Pakistan and Global Nuclear Disarmament.* New York: Olive Branch Press, 2000.

Butalia, Urvashi. *The Other Side of Silence: Views from the Partition of India.* Durham, NC: Duke University Press, 2000.

Chester, Lucy. "Parting of the ways," *History Today.* March 2000.

Edwards, Michael. *Nehru: A Political Biography.* New York: Praeger Publishers, 1971.

Ginsberg, Thomas. "War on terror reignites India-Pakistan dispute," *Philadelphia Inquirer,* January 13, 2002, p. A18.

Gupte, Pranay. *Mother India: A Political Biography of Indira Gandhi.* New York: Charles Scribner's Sons, 1992.

Harrison, Selig S., Kreisberg, Paul H. and Kux, Dennis (eds.). *India and Pakistan: The First Fifty Years.* Washington, DC: Woodrow Wilson Center Press, 1999.

McGirk, Tim. "Making the final cut," *Time,* Vol. 150, No. 6, August 11, 1997.

Moraes, Dom. *Indira Gandhi.* Boston: Little, Brown & Co., 1980.

Read, Anthony and Fisher, David. *The Proudest Day: India's Long Road to Independence.* New York: W.W. Norton & Co., 1997.

Tellis, Ashley J. *Stability in South Asia.* Santa Monica, CA: RAND, 1997.

Tinker, Hugh. *India and Pakistan.* New York: Praeger Publishers, 1962.

Williams, L.F. Rushbrook. *The State of Pakistan.* London: Faber and Faber, 1962.

Ziring, Lawrence. *Pakistan in the Twentieth Century.* New York: Oxford University Press, 1997.

WEB SITES:

Britannica.com

CNN.com

Countrywatch.com

Nic.in

Pak.gov.pk

Pakobserver.com

Times.com

Timesofindia.com

Washingtonpost.com

page:

6: Courtesy of the U.S. Central
Intelligence Agency
8: Getty Images
16: Getty Images
19: Associated Press, AP
22: Associated Press, AP
25: Courtesy of the U.S. Central
Intelligence Agency
27: Associated Press, AP
33: Associated Press, AP
35: © Bettmann/Corbis
39: © Bettmann/Corbis
43: Getty Images
47: © Bettmann/Corbis
51: Associated Press, AP
54: Getty Images

57: Associated Press, AP
61: Associated Press, AP
65: Associated Press, AP
69: Getty Images
71: Getty Images
74: © Bettmann/Corbis
77: Getty Images
80: Getty Images
83: Associated Press, AP
86: Associated Press, AP
90: Associated Press, AP
93: Associated Press, AP
97: Associated Press, AP
99: Associated Press, AP
102: Associated Press, AP

HEATHER LEHR WAGNER is a writer and editor. She earned an M.A. in government from the College of William and Mary and a B.A. in political science from Duke University. She is the author of several books for teens on global and family issues. She is also the author of *Israel and the Arab World* and *The IRA and England* in the People at Odds series.